HERALD SCRIPTURAL LIBRARY
Robert J. Karris O.F.M., *General Editor*

BUILDING CHRIST'S BODY

The Dynamics of Christian Living According to St. Paul

by

George T. Montague S.M.

FRANCISCAN HERALD PRESS
Chicago, Illinois 60609

Building Christ's Body: The Dynamics of Christian Living According to St. Paul by George T. Montague S.M., Herald Scriptural Library, General Editor, Robert J. Karris O.F.M., copyright ©1975, Franciscan Herald Press, 1434 West 51st Street, Chicago, Illinois 60609.

Library of Congress Cataloging in Publication Data
Montague, George T.
 Building Christ's body.
 (Herald scriptural library)
 Bibliography: p.
 1. Christian life—Biblical teaching. 2. Paul,
Saint, apostle. I. Title.
BS2655.C4M66   248'.4   75-14100
ISBN 0-8199-0573-9

Nihil Obstat:
MARK HEGENER O.F.M.
Censor Deputatus

Imprimatur:
MSGR. RICHARD A. ROSEMEYER, J.D.
Vicar General, Archdiocese of Chicago

"The Nihil Obstat and Imprimatur are official declarations that a book or pamphlet is free of doctrinal error. No implication is contained therein that those who have granted the Nihil Obstat and the Imprimatur agree with the contents, opinions, or statements expressed."

MADE IN THE UNITED STATES OF AMERICA

TABLE OF CONTENTS

INTRODUCTION

IN recent years there has been a marked revival of interest in the Christian life as personal biography. Whether through the influence of existentialism or a new thirst for experiential Christianity and mysticism, this development has been a return to a long-standing tradition, from the *Confessions* of Augustine to *The Seven-Storey Mountain* of Merton. Augustine already discovered the immense spiritual importance of memory in his personal salvation history, and long before him the Bible was there, constructing meaning for the people of God from the great events of their corporate memory.

Is it possible to reconstruct a spiritual biography for the apostle Paul? Our only sources, the Acts and Paul's letters, were admittedly never written for such a purpose. The reminiscences of Acts have been heavily retouched by Luke to serve his catechetical purpose. And Paul's letters are for the most part not a personal correspondence but a public response to the unpredictable emerging needs of the early communities. Hardly the kind of stuff likely to come out of a recluse's study!

And yet, when Paul's letters are read in their historical setting and sequence, the elements of his own spiritual development are clearly detectable. He comes to appreciate what his own union with Christ means at ever deeper levels of his personal experience, and, in response to the pastoral needs in his communities, he is led to develop an ever richer theological synthesis. For anyone trying to lead a Christian life

3

and serve others in some form of Christian ministry, following Paul's spiritual itinerary is an invaluable experience.

Our purpose here, then, is to discover the dynamics of the Christian life according to Paul. Our method will be to follow the chronology of Paul's life and ministry and the chronology of the letters as best we can determine it. The obvious limitation of this method is that it leaves synthesis largely to the reader and runs some risk of repetition. But the advantages, the author is convinced, amply compensate, for we are kept closer to the text of the New Testament in its context and we have a greater chance of learning about the Christian life as an ongoing experience or, if you will, as a journey.

One might compare the method even more fruitfully to the climbing of a mountain. As one begins the ascent, certain aspects of the landscape loom large and command attention. The longer one climbs and the higher one goes, new elements of the landscape emerge and the earlier ones recede into a more general view. So it will be in studying Paul inductively. Elements introduced in the early letters rarely leave him entirely, but as his attention is drawn to other elements in the gospel message, original insights become tempered by an ever wider panorama. So it is with our own experience of life. So it was with Paul.

Chapter One

THE CALL AND THE CHANGE

Suggested readings: Acts 9:1-30; 22:5-16; 26:12-20; Gal 1:11-17; Phil 3:3-14; 2 Cor 4:6.

THE synoptics and John relate instances of both call and conversion, but it is clear that the two are not exactly the same. Jesus calls Peter and Andrew, James and John, and they leave their nets and their business and follow him. There is no suggestion in these "vocation" texts that these fishermen were turning from lives of great sin. What they left was their nets and, in the case of James and John, their father. Obviously they were taking up a new life, but the word "conversion" hardly applies to the experience by the lakeshore when Jesus walked by and invited them to follow him.

According to Luke, though Peter is aware of his sinfulness from the earliest hour (Lk 5:8), his deepest experience of conversion came long after his call, when he repented of his denial of Jesus: "When you have converted, strengthen your brethren" (Lk 22:32). Conversion, then, is not simply the same thing as calling, for the calling of the first disciples was not conversion.

The same may be concluded from John's portrait of the first disciples' following of Jesus (Jn 1:35-51). Even more than the synoptics, John highlights the element of invitation and mystery: "Rabbi, where do you dwell?" they ask. "Come

5

and see," Jesus replies. The fact that these first disciples were disciples of John the Baptist no doubt implied that they had already received the "baptism of repentance for the forgiveness of sins." Following Jesus, then, was less a turning from sin than a turning to the one who fulfilled the promise they were awaiting.

There are also examples in the gospels of conversion without calling to the itinerant discipleship. The woman taken in adultery is simply told to go her way and sin no more (Jn 8:3-11) The paralytic is forgiven, cured and sent home (Mk 2:11). The Gerasene demoniac is healed and delivered but he is forbidden to follow Jesus (Mk 5:19). Zacchaeus' life is radically changed, but it is not said that he followed Jesus (Lk 19:1-10).

On the other hand, it occasionally happens that a call is, by implication, a conversion. Jesus' calling of the tax-collector Levi follows the same pattern as the earlier callings by the lakeside. But when Levi throws a party for Jesus and invites other tax-collectors, Jesus meets the needling question of the Pharisees with the words, "I have not come to call the righteous, but sinners to repentance" (Lk 5:27-32). By implication, Levi and his friends were "sinners," and the scandal was that Jesus would not only eat with them but that he would even choose an intimate disciple from among them. Levi had apparently not received John's baptism of repentance; following Jesus' call then must have meant for him a conversion of life equivalent to and perhaps exceeding that of John's disciples. In other words, where repentance to prepare for the kingdom had not already occurred (Mk 1:15), it was implied in the response to Jesus' call.

If the notion of "conversion" is not to be confused with that of "calling," even more so is it to be distinguished from other notions such as election, appointment or sending. Out of the many disciples who followed Jesus Mark tells us he chose and appointed some to be with him and to be sent out to preach (Mk 3:13).

Luke's View of Paul's Conversion

These remarks will be helpful when it comes to considering how Luke in Acts views the momentous event on the road to Damascus. The story of Paul is so central to Luke's history of the early Church that he can practically consider everything that happened as belonging to two periods: that of Peter (up to chapter 12), and that of Paul (chapter 12 to the end). Under the rubric of Peter, the gospel that Jesus had brought from Galilee to Jerusalem is carried to Judea and Samaria. Under the rubric of Paul it reaches "the ends of the earth," Rome (cf. Acts 1:8). And within the story of Paul, the account of Paul's amazing reversal from persecutor to apostle is so important that he narrates it three times, first as his own report (9:1-19), then twice on the lips of Paul (22:1-21; 26:1-23).

What is Luke up to, and how do the "conversion stories" in Acts relate to his purpose? Luke deserves the title historian not primarily because he claims to have ferreted out documents and data from the earliest hour (Lk 1:1-4) but above all because he is the *interpreter* of the experience of primitive Christianity. That is, he has taken isolated events, many of which appeared utterly chaotic and disruptive, and found an order among them and hence a meaning. Take for example the gentile mission. For many Jewish Christians this was experienced as utter chaos, as the overturning of practices which they held sacred, as a cheap flattening of the original Jewish matrix of Christianity to fit just anybody into the holy people of God. Luke had to show that the gentile mission was not really in discontinuity with the best of Judaism. Especially did he want to show that the irruption of Paul into the early Church was not really the breach it may have seemed to many of Paul's contemporaries. Now this was no easy task, for Luke's readers knew as well as he that Paul could not qualify as one of the witnesses who had been with Jesus since the time of John the Baptist (Acts 1:22). By what authority, then, could Paul lead the Church into wholesale evangelization of the gentiles — with the relaxations he permitted them? Aside from their purpose as reports, the conversion stories aim to answer that burning question.

A simple reading of the first account bears out Luke's interest. He shows how unprepared Paul was for this experience (vs. 3) and how it completely paralyzed him for three days (vs. 8). At the heart of this account, as of the other two, is the dialogue, and the fact that there is verbal agreement in all three accounts on the words exchanged shows how central the dialogue is. It is by word and command of the Lord Jesus himself that Paul is transformed from persecutor to obedient servant (vss. 4-6). He is made obedient to the community he has persecuted, for he will be instructed like everyone else (vs. 6). Although Luke respects the mystery of the theophany here and does not say explicitly that Paul *saw* Jesus, the conclusion is inescapable both from the bright light (vs. 3) and Paul's consequent blindness (vs. 8), which should be understood not as a punishment but as a natural consequence of encounter with the divine light. Although Luke is loathe to apply the term *apostle* to Paul (he knows that the "twelve" are unique), it is clear that Paul has seen the risen Lord as really as the primitive disciples did. Paul himself will not hesitate to say that this suffices to accredit him as an apostle (1 Cor 9:1; 15:5). The fears expressed by Ananias (vs. 13) clearly anticipate the well-founded fears of the Jerusalem church (vs. 26), but these are allayed by a command from Jesus himself (let the Jerusalem church hear!). Moreover, Paul's appointment to service for the Lord is an ordination not to glory but to suffering (vs. 15f), and this could hardly have been a vocation of Paul's choosing! Finally (vss. 17, 18) Ananias ministers to Paul and Paul is baptized. Since the rite symbolized not only union with Jesus but repentance, Paul's entrance into the community is a real conversion and not simply a call to a higher state of life.

Luke's interest in telling this story makes it impossible for us to fully satisfy our curiosity as to the meaning of this event subjectively for Paul. Luke's concern is not with the inward experience of conversion but with the fact that the Lord himself felled the Church's most powerful adversary and brought him into the Christian camp. This much is clear: Paul's entrance into the ranks of the Lord's servants was not his own idea — it was at the invitation of Jesus the Lord.

The second account (22:1-21) sharpens these elements, as Paul himself takes up his defense — in Aramaic! "I am a Jew," he begins. The setting, the language and the message all justify seeing the emphasis fall on "I am" — not "I was" or even "I have been." The sense is "I am right now an authentic Jew." The light of the vision becomes here "a *great* light" (vs. 6) and verse 11 makes clear that Paul's blindness was not a punishment but rather simply the effect of having seen Christ in *glory*. The importance of this note should not be lost on the Christian reader: such a vision with such an effect is not attributed to anyone else in the New Testament before or after the Ascension. The event of the transfiguration does not quite compare, and the post-Resurrection appearances are not blinding ones. Hence, although Paul may not be able to claim equality with the original disciples, only he has seen the Lord in his blinding glory. In this sense he is like a new Moses (and Paul himself will exploit the parallel in 2 Cor 4:4-6).

Ananias, who welcomes Paul into the Church, is an ideal

Jew (vs. 12). Paul's sins, like everyone else's, are remitted
in baptism (vs. 16). He is not therefore a "super-Christian."
Christ's command to go to the gentiles receives added emphasis from its setting in the temple itself as Paul prayed
there as a devout Jew (vs. 17). Moreover, the Lord's command is occasioned by the disbelief of the Jews themselves
(vs. 21).

The crowd reacts violently only at the moment that the
mission to the gentiles is proclaimed (again let the Jewish
church hear, lest it become like the disbelievers!). Paul in
his discourse never answers the original accusation of having
brought a gentile into the temple. Luke has used this detail
symbolically. While it is obvious Paul has not physically
brought a gentile into the temple court, he has opened the
doors of God's house to all gentiles — but only because the
Lord himself had commanded it!

The third account (26:1-23) re-emphasizes the points
made in the previous ones and then climaxes with an original
theological insight. It is explicitly clear that Paul has seen the
risen Lord (vs. 16). And he is on trial not because of his
specifically Christian belief but because of his *Jewish* belief!
(vs. 6). To be a Christian is therefore consonant with being
a Pharisee. The absurdity is that the Jews brought Paul to
trial precisely because of their most cherished hopes (vs. 7).
And Paul insists that what he preaches is nothing beyond the
promise contained in Moses and the prophets (vss. 22, 23).
Then in verses 16-18, Paul introduces and applies to himself
a cluster of Old Testament texts that describe the calls of
prophets. The words "rise and stand on your feet," come
straight from Ez 2:1, 2, words addressed by the Lord to
Ezekiel at the prophet's inaugural call. "To open their eyes"
(vs. 18) evokes what was said of the prophet-servant of the
Lord in Is 42:7, 16, and the expression "I have delivered
you" recalls the inaugural vision of Jeremiah (1:7, 8). In

Luke's eyes, then, Paul is a prophet and indeed the one in whom the prophecies made of the Servant of Yahweh with regard to the gentiles are fulfilled.

This becomes clear when we compare Luke 4:18, 19 with Matthew 12:18-21. Both texts concern the mission of the servant upon whom the Spirit of the Lord rests. Matthew quotes Is 42:1-4, which mentions a mission to the gentiles. Luke selects instead a different text from Isaiah (61:1, 2), one which omits mention of the gentiles. Luke is aware that it was not Jesus himself but only the apostolic Church that actually brought the mission to the gentiles. The text Matthew used of the public life of Jesus Luke does finally use but only in Acts, applying it to Paul. Behind all this is Luke's subtle trump card. The Jerusalem church elaborated its understanding of Jesus in terms of the Servant of Yahweh. Very well, Luke says; but there is one element about that prophecy which was not fulfilled in Jesus and was fulfilled in Paul: the bringing of the good news of salvation to the gentiles. Paul is thus associated with Jesus most intimately, even though he is not one of the twelve: Jesus cannot be the Servant of Yahweh bringing salvation to the gentiles without Paul. Paul's work is not therefore deviation: it is fulfillment.

The accounts of Paul's conversion thus have a particular purpose in Luke. It is natural that Luke would stress the continuity of Paul with Judaism and tone down the violent disagreement with the Jewish interpretation of the law which we find in his letters. In Luke, Paul is still a good Pharisee: "I am a Pharisee, the son of Pharisees" (Acts 23:6). Surprising as this may be when we remember the "unredeemed" picture Luke has painted of the Pharisees in his Gospel (e.g. 18:9-14), it shows that for Luke there is a basic continuity between the purest of Judaism and the Christian faith.

Paul's View

Paul's own view of his conversion agrees in part with Luke's and yet diverges from it in important respects. Three major texts give us Paul's view of his experience:

Galatians 1:1 1-17

For I would have you know, brethren, that the gospel which was preached by me is not man's gospel. For I did not receive it from man, nor was I taught it, but it came through a revelation of Jesus Christ. For you have heard of my former life in Judaism, how I persecuted the church of God violently and tried to destroy it; and I advanced in Judaism beyond many of my own age among my people, so extremely zealous was I for the traditions of my fathers.

But when he who had set me apart before I was born, and had called me through his grace, was pleased to reveal his Son to me, in order that I might preach him among the Gentiles, I did not confer with flesh and blood, nor did I go up to Jerusalem to those who were apostles before me, but I went away into Arabia; and again I returned to Damascus. (RSV)

Philippians 3:3-14

For we are the true circumcision, who worship God in spirit, and glory in Christ Jesus, and put no confidence in the flesh. Though I myself have reason for confidence in the flesh also. If any other man thinks he has reason for confidence in the flesh, I have more: circumcised on the eighth day, of the people of Israel, of the tribe of Benjamin, a Hebrew born of Hebrews; as to the law a Pharisee, as to zeal a persecutor of the church, as to righteousness under the law blameless. But whatever gain I had, I counted a loss for the sake of Christ. Indeed I count everything as loss because of the surpassing worth of knowing Christ Jesus my Lord. For his sake I have suffered the loss of all things, and count them as refuse, in order that I may gain Christ and be found in him, not having a righteousness of my own, based on law, but that which is through faith in Christ, the righteousness from God that depends on faith; that I may know him and the power of his resurrection, and may share his sufferings, becoming like him in his death, that if possible I may attain the resurrection from the dead.

Not that I have already obtained this or am already perfect. No — I press on, hoping to overtake and capture — since that is just what Christ Jesus has done to me. Brothers, I do not consider myself already to have won. But one thing I do: forgetting what lies behind and straining toward what lies ahead, I press on toward the goal, to the prize of God's heavenward calling in Christ Jesus. (RSV)

2 Corinthians 4:6
For God, who said, "Let light shine out of darkness," has shone in our hearts, that we in turn might make known the glory of God shining on the face of Christ. (NAB)

We have no alternative but to accept the fact that in each of these passages Paul is engaged in a polemic. He never set out, as Augustine did, to write a "personal salvation history." It is only when he has to muster all his energies to settle the issue of what the gospel is really about that he calls upon his own personal experience. And even here he is interested in speaking about his conversion only because it typifies, in his mind at least, the authentic and universal Christian experience: faith in Christ Jesus. Though Gal 1:16 is often translated "to reveal his son to me," the Greek literally says "*in* me" — that is, the Church may learn from Paul's whole life, and not just from his teaching, who Jesus is. Precisely for that reason Paul's conversion experience has for us not merely a historical interest but a theological one as well.

We recognize at once in these texts some of the elements we have already encountered in Luke's later interpretation of the event. The element of suddenness and surprise appears in Paul's description of his conversion as being "seized" or "captured" by Christ (Phil 3:12). Elsewhere Paul will say that his entry into the apostolic college was like a birth out of due time (literally, a "miscarriage," 1 Cor 15:8). His credentials as a Jew and a devout Pharisee are paraded (Gal 1:13, 14; Phil 3:4-6). The glory on the face of Christ Jesus is a glowing memory and a foretaste of the heavenly glory to which all Christians are called (2 Cor 4:6; 2 Th 1:9; 1 Cor 13:12). The good news came not from man but from God; Paul did not learn it as a rabbi might learn in a school but rather as a prophet learns through a revelation (Gal 1:12, 16). In Gal 1:15, 16 Paul evokes the inaugural calls of Jeremiah (Jer 1:5) and of the Servant of the Lord (Is 49:1) and goes on to apply the latter text to his mission to the gentiles (cf. Is 49:6). In these elements of the interpretation Luke has been faithful to Paul's self-portrait.

But unlike Luke, Paul saw his conversion as a conversion *from* Pharisaism. It was a real break with his whole previous approach to life — God, others, and self. He insists with vehemence that he is not a Christ-coated Pharisee nor even a Pharisee come to full term. He is an entirely new creation (2 Cor 5:17).

The pre-Christian Paul that Paul the Christian was rejecting was certainly not Paul the Jew. Nobody but a Jew could have written Romans. Paul loved his people so much that he could entertain the thought of losing Christ himself if they could but have him (Rom 9:1-5). And certainly it was not the peculiarly Pharisaic belief in the resurrection of the just that Paul rejected. It was rather *his own particular brand of Pharisaism,* and that requires some explanation.

The Pharisees were not a political party but an essentially religious one, and this explains not only their power and duration but also their attractiveness to the people. Though constituting not more perhaps than five percent of the population, they were admired even by those who did not care to imitate them. Their origins went back to Maccabean times, to the Hasidim ("the pious" or "the loyalists") who had manifested their fidelity to the Jewish faith and to the law in spite of bitter persecution. Under John Hyrcanus they appeared primarily as teachers of the law. They sought to interpret and apply the law to the many cases of daily life which the law had not explicitly envisaged. They sought to give authority to their interpretations not only by the texts of the law itself but also by appealing to a body of rabbinic traditions with which the law had become embroidered. Their authority derived therefore not from the high priest nor from the people but from "the traditions of the fathers" — and hence, in the last analysis, from their own knowledge. They became thus the learned elite and were dubbed "Pharisees," that is "separated." Separated from what? From the common people unlearned in the law.

This separation would not have been so acute had the Pharisees not been convinced that a thorough knowledge of the law was necessary for the observance of it. Ignorance of the law was really no excuse. Now the common people, ignorant of the finer details of the law, no doubt transgressed it frequently and thus incurred legal defilement. According to the prevailing interpretation, legal defilement was incurred not only by the transgressor but also by anyone who came into contact with him. And sharing a meal was a most likely form of contracting such defilement. For this reason the safer course by far for the Pharisee was to avoid all contact with the *ham ha-aretz,* these "people of the land," the common and unlearned. This safer practice became a sacred rule for the Pharisees, who originally called themselves "the loyalists" but ended by accepting the title *Pharisees,* which implied their separation from the common and the ignorant. Toward these the attitude of many a Pharisee was a distrust which easily led to suspicion and then to condemnation and disdain. "The man who is not learned," said the great rabbi Hillel, "has no fear of sin; the common people cannot be pious" (*Aboth* II, 6).

Saul the Pharisee fits this picture very well: "As far as the law was concerned, I was a Pharisee" (Phil 3:5), as if to say, "What more could I have been?" And in Gal 1:14: "And I advanced in Judaism above many of my contemporaries in my nation, showing much more zeal for the traditions of my fathers." This was Paul's life project, his ideal in life, and he accurately describes its glories in Rom 2:17-20: "You call yourself a Jew. You rely on the law and boast of your relation to God. You know his will and approve what is excellent, because you are instructed in the law. You are sure that you are a guide to the blind, a light to those who are in darkness, a corrector of the foolish, a teacher of children, having in the law the embodiment of knowledge and truth." But the "law" which Saul the Pharisees knew was so vast it could be learned only by the scholar. His aim was to know it, to observe meticulously its most minor precepts according to the strict Pharisaical tradition (a matter which, naturally, could be "controlled" and thus afforded the security of the "check-list"), and a vigilant separation from the common people who might defile his legal purity.

This attitude explains to a great extent the reaction of Saul the Pharisee to the early Jesus-followers. They were a sect within Judaism made up largely of the common people who rallied around a Galilean who because of his undue liberties with the law got himself crucified and thus supremely cursed by the law (Dt 21:23). What else did they deserve but contempt and hatred? They deserved more: Whereas Saul seemed to feel no impulse to open war against other sects in Judaism (the Sadducees or the Zealots or the Essenes), he could not tolerate a sect of this type. For, by taking their own leader more seriously than the law, its adherents were really making a religion of their own ignorance. They were, moreover, winning converts at a rapid pace, even among the learned elite. They were a threat to the law itself, and hence to God. And once Saul had made that connection, there was nothing to keep him from taking the next step: Saul the Pharisee became Saul the persecutor.

The event on the Damascus road was cataclysmic. Still, it was not a total erasure of Paul's Jewish theology and tradition. True conversion is never spiritual lobotomy, and Paul's was certainly not. There is something that remains when everything else changes. What remained with Paul was his keen desire to know God and to do his will. As a Pharisee he had simply assumed that knowing (and observing) the law was equivalent to knowing God. After all, the Torah itself taught that no man can see God and live (Ex 33:20); and it offered itself as the substitute for the direct knowledge of God. Moses may have seen God's glory on the mount but every other Israelite could know him only through the law (Ex 19:21-20:21). By doing God's will, one "knew God" (Jer 22:15, 16). The more exact the knowledge of the law and the more extensive the observance, the more perfectly did one "know God" and the more certain was one's justification in his sight. So believed Saul the Pharisee. But now the glory of God had been revealed in the "face of Christ Jesus" (2 Cor 4:6). God is known not via law, even his own, but via a person, his Son! Paul defines his ambition no longer as aiming "to know the law" (Rom 2:18) but seeking "to know Christ, and the power of his resurrection and the fellowship of his sufferings" (Phil 3:10). And the God who reveals himself in Jesus Christ is not the publisher and reminder of performance-expectations as if to his slaves but he who calls in and through the gracious gift of his Son (Gal 1:6), that is, he is "Abba!" (Gal 4:6; Rom 8:15), the Jewish term of intimate affection akin to our "Daddy!", a name never used by Jews to address God. And if the Christian calls God his dearest Father, then it follows that "You are no longer a slave but a son!" (Gal 4:7). If it is true that nothing so influences one's spiritual life as one's image of God, then the new name by which Paul addresses God marks a radical shift in his whole spiritual experience not only of God but of himself, others and the world.

We are really, of course, getting ahead of our story and calling on texts in which Paul later developed the meaning of the new life in Christ. Suffice it to note at this point simply that Paul, unlike Luke, stresses his discontinuity with Pharisaic Judaism because most of his contemporaries really did not see that the gospel of Jesus Christ made any radical difference from Judaism, which had always been open to a spectrum of life-styles around the Torah as core. Paul's uniqueness lies in the stress he places on the whole Christian life as the *gift* of God accepted in faith — in diametrical opposition to his own previous assessment of righteousness as a matter of works. His own call by Christ illustrates that God's gift is not a matter of rewarding a man's works, for Paul's "works" were really aimed against God's will. Paul's call was, as much as any sinner's, a conversion. But it was not repentance from the kind of sins of the flesh which were gentile fare. Rather it was from the sin of trying to make his own "justification," to prove himself lovable to God, and to himself, in preference to receiving God's gift that would make him lovable. It was being fixated on giving and proving, when God wanted him to receive and experience.

For that basically is the difference Jesus makes. "I do not cast away the *gift* of God, for if justification is by the law, then Christ died in vain" (Gal 2:21; cf. 5:4,11). God's gift means God's love manifested in the self-gift of Jesus on the cross (Gal 1:4; 2:20,21; Rom 8:39), confirmed by the Resurrection and enthronement of Jesus as Lord (Rom 1:4) and poured into the hearts of Christians by the Holy Spirit (Rom 5:5). From beginning to end, the Christian life is God's *gift* in Christ Jesus our Lord (Rom 6:23), a gift one cannot experience if one prefers anything else, be it even the law!

Here lies the radical newness of Paul the Christian. It was not even so much the person of Christ Jesus that made the difference, for the Judaizing Christians also apparently accepted Jesus as the Messiah and perhaps even called him "Lord." The difference lay in what the experience of Jesus and the Spirit now meant for the law, specifically for the whole attitude of "meeting performance expectations" which had been Paul's and was now the attitude even of his Jewish-Christian opponents. That attitude, Paul was convinced, was incompatible with being a Christian. For it was irreconcilable with the *gift* of God in Jesus. And if the cross illustrated this newness on God's part, Paul's own conversion story illustrated it on his: "He called me by his grace" (Gal 1:15), and "I am the least of the apostles, unfit to be called an apostle, because I persecuted the Church of God. By the *grace* of God, however, I am what I am, and his *grace* unto me has not been fruitless" (1 Cor 15:10).

Chapter Two

UNTIL THE LORD COMES

Suggested readings: Acts 13:1-18:17; 1 and 2 Thessalonians

BETWEEN the blinding moment on the road to Damascus and the writing of the first letter we have from Paul's hand, some 15 years elapse. Luke's picture of what happened during that time is related in Acts 13-18. After his retreat in the Arabian desert Paul remained for a while in Damascus, then came to Jerusalem to consult with Peter and James, and finally returned to his hometown of Tarsus, where at length Barnabas came to fetch him and attach him to the community of Antioch.

A first missionary journey into Asia Minor took him to Cyprus, Pisidian Antioch, Lystra and Derbe. It was probably after this journey that he participated in the discussion in Jerusalem which settled the attitude to be adopted concerning pagan converts (Acts 15:5-29). A second journey, this time with Silas (Acts 15:40), brought him overland, through the communities he had founded on the earlier visit, to Troas on the western coast of Asia Minor. There as a result of a vision the missionaries crossed to Macedonia (Acts 16:9, 10) and brought the gospel to Europe. The first community founded was at Philippi, made up largely of pagan converts. It was after Paul's imprisonment there that he came to Thessalonica. Here there was a Jewish synagogue. Acts 17 continues (2-9):

Following his usual custom, Paul joined the people there and conducted discussions with them about the Scriptures for three sabbaths. He explained many things, showing that the Messiah had to suffer and rise from the dead: "This Jesus I am telling you about is the Messiah!" Some of the Jews were convinced and threw in their lot with Paul and Silas. So, too, did a great number of Greeks sympathetic to Judaism, and numerous prominent women.

This only aroused the resentment of the Jews, however, who engaged loafers from the public square to form a mob and start a riot in the town. They marched on the house of Jason in an attempt to bring Paul and Silas before the people's assembly. When they could not find them there, they dragged Jason himself and some of the brothers to the town magistrates, shouting: "These men have been creating a disturbance all over the place. Now they come here and Jason has taken them in. To a man, they disregard the Emperor's decrees and claim instead that a certain Jesus is king." In this way they stirred up the crowd. When the town's magistrates heard the whole story, they released Jason and the others on bail. (NAB)

Luke in his habitual manner has telescoped Paul's ministry at Thessalonica, probably by describing the beginning (vv. 1-4) and the end (vv. 5-9). Considering the evidence of the first letter to the Thessalonians, it is probable that after a failure with the Jews Paul concentrated upon evangelizing the gentiles, and surely for more than "three sabbaths," perhaps as much as three months. The impression given by vs. 4 is one of considerable success: around a core of Jews, a large number of "god-fearing Greeks," and a number of prominent women in the city. When we remember that first century Judiasm, particularly in the diaspora, reached out actively to make converts from among the gentiles, we can understand

how, around the Jewish community of Thessalonica gravi-
tated a number of Greeks sympathetic to Judaism. Equally
understandable, then, would be the resentment of those Jews
who were disturbed at Paul's success, particularly among
these people who were their greatest sympathizers. Paul was,
in their view, a seriously divisive trouble-maker, and it was
important at all costs to get rid of him. Luke gives us some
indication how this came about, but since his primary interest
is the lot of Paul, he leaves us only to guess at the tense situation in which the infant Christian community had to live after
Paul's departure. This situation of struggle at the founding
hours of the community as well as in its continuing experience is echoed in almost every line of the two letters to the
Thessalonians. Paul writes them from Corinth, where he had
established himself after a brief and largely unsuccessful
mission in Athens.

The Lord's Coming

These two letters, which we shall consider together because
they are so close both in chronology and doctrine, could be
facetiously entitled, "How to Hang on Until the Lord Comes."
Their central doctrinal focus is the Lord's second coming.

Because every aspect of the Christian life, including its
growth, is seen in the light of this final and dramatic closing
of history, we must give a bit of its background, particularly
since the apocalyptic world-view differs so much from our
contemporary experience.

Central to Old Testament faith is the conviction that the
Lord God, Yahweh, is a God who acts in history. The most
primitive conception of "Yahweh Sabaoth," the "Lord of
Armies," is that of a tribal God who reveals his power and
loyalty to his people on the battlefield. After the conquest of
Palestine this conception continued, but through the work of
the prophets, the Lord's covenant loyalty becomes highly

conditioned upon Israel's reciprocal loyalty, which was spelled out in terms of clear ethical expectations. Thus, whether it was the event of Sennacherib's amazing retreat from the walls of Jerusalem, which Isaiah had promised to King Hezekiah if the King would simply manifest his faith in Yahweh (2 Kgs 19), or the Babylonian conquest of Jerusalem which Jeremiah interpreted, already before it happened, as Yahweh's punishment for Israel's infidelity, history continued to be the mirror in which Israel interpreted her relationship with the Lord.

After the exile, however, the adequacy of this mirror to interpret her life underwent serious questioning from two different wings of Judaism. From the Wisdom wing came works like Job and Qoheleth (Ecclesiastes), which questioned, either in terms of one man's personal experience, as in the case of Job, or in terms of general principles, as in the case of Qoheleth, whether one could adequately read man's relationship to God in terms of the events of human history. Is it really always true that material happiness and prosperity mean God's approval and adversity God's punishment? Out of the apocalyptic wing, forged under the fires of persecution, came not only the same question but an answer: human history, as man experiences it presently, does not achieve a balance of reward for good and punishment for evil. How, then, can God manifest his justice and settle all scores? How, in short, can Yahweh still be the victorious God Israel's fathers had believed in? When and how does he win? It is no longer adequate to say that somehow he works within human history by raising up Babylonians to wipe out Assyrians or Romans to conquer Greeks. It can only be by a cosmic intervention in which the God of heaven and earth himself takes over the stage of human history and has "his day." It will be the end of history as we know it and the beginning of the "reign of God." Thus appears the distinction in Judaism between the "present age," full of ambiguities, and "the age to come," which is perfect and ultimate (technically called, "eschatological"). Several terms are used to describe this "age to come." It is the "reign of God" or "the kingdom of God." It is the "day of the Lord," a day in which sinners experience his judgment and his faithful ones, the saints, his glory.

For Paul the "kingdom of God" and the "day of the Lord" are used to describe the event of the Second Coming of Christ, a day which will reveal the works of darkness for what they are and bring them to an end and similarly bring glory and final vindication to the just. But Paul uses another term for this final event, one borrowed from the Hellenistic world: the *Parousia*. It can be translated, "presence," "appearance," "visitation," or "coming." It was a technical term in the Hellenistic world for the visitation of a city or a province by the Emperor whose appearance was thought to be a "manifestation of divinity." The city or province would prepare at great length for this reception, and upon the Emperor's approach to the city, the city officials and often the entire populace would go to meet him outside the city gates and lead him processionally into the city. In addition to being a grandiose celebration, such a visit was often the occasion for redressing certain wrongs or determining sanctions. For Christians who had witnessed such an event perhaps once in their lifetime, or had heard tell of it, the scene would be a meaningful way to describe the victorious return of Jesus and his manifestation as Lord. For the Hellenistic Jew the image of Parousia was an easy Hellenization of the Jewish concepts of the kingdom of God and the day of the Lord.

Parousia and Resurrection

For us the Second Coming of Christ is often like a vague postscript to what we consider his most important manifestation, the Resurrection, which is past. For Paul and the early Christians, at least at the time of the writing of the epistles to the Thessalonians, the relationship between the Parousia and the Resurrection is just the reverse. The great event under whose power one lives as a Christian is the coming of the Lord. The Resurrection of Jesus is seen primarily as a guarantee and an anticipation of this coming cosmic event. Such is the view that emerges quite clearly from 1 Thes 1:9,10, where the Christian life is defined as a commitment to "serve a living and true God, and to wait for his Son from heaven, whom he raised from the dead, Jesus who delivers us from the wrath to come" (see also Acts 17:31; 3:20). This is not, of course, Paul's last word about the Resurrection, but it is his first, and it is interesting to note how the passing of fifteen years since his vision of the risen Lord on the road to Damascus, has not weakened his conviction that because Jesus is risen, he is coming. Thus the primary image of Jesus which he has before him is not the risen Lord of Easter morning but the coming Lord of the last day. A quick glance at the number of passages in which the Parousia is express or implicit shows how central this preoccupation is: besides the text of 1 Thes 1:10, already cited, there are the long passages in which Paul discusses matters related to the last day: 1 Thes 4:13-18 on the share that the Christian dead will have in the glory of the Lord's coming; 1 Thes 5:1-11 on readiness for the day; 2 Thes 1:5-11 on the certainty of the day, 2:1-12 on the signs preceding the day. Then there are passing allusions to the Parousia (1 Thes 3:13; 5:23) or to God's kingdom and glory or the glory of Jesus Christ to which the Christians are called (2 Thes 1:5,11; 2:14).

The Christian Life

How does this view affect the present Christian life lived under the expectation of the Lord's coming? The community is described as one awaiting the Lord. It is "the church of the Thessalonians in God our Father and the Lord Jesus Christ" (1 Thes 1:1). Behind the Greek word *ekklesia* stands the Hebrew *qahal Yahweh,* the "assembly of the Lord" in the desert. Even more strongly than the Hebrew, the Greek word suggests a group of people called out for some purpose, usually a public meeting. In the specific context of Thessalonians, Christians are called out of the world to await the appearance of the Lord Jesus in glory. There is no doubt that this bespeaks a discontinuity of the Christian community with the world in which it lives. It is quite clearly a community whose ultimate purpose is beyond time and history. Some of the Thessalonians had concluded from this fact that they should become loafers and thus not be doing anything when the Lord would arrive. A gross misunderstanding of what it means to await the Lord! If the Christian Church does present a discontinuity with this present world, it does not cease to be active in it. More concretely, time is something to be used and to be redeemed for the Lord (2 Thes 3:6-15). This is a crucial point. It will distinguish Christianity from religions that would foster contemplation at the expense of withdrawal from the world.

For all of that, however, the Church is the community of the final times gathered to await the Lord's return to glory. Stamped with this indelible identity, the church of the Thessalonians suffers in order to preserve it. As Paul experienced opposition in the early preaching at Thessalonica (1 Thes 2:2), so the early community received the good news in the midst of great trials (1 Thes 1:6), a situation that has continued (1 Thes 2:14-16; 3:3,4; 2 Thes 1:4-10). In this situation Paul sees the development of the Christian life first of all in the direction of strengthening and stabilizing the community. This is why he sends Timothy for this purpose (1 Thes 3:1-5), why he feels a need to complete their Christian instruction (1 Thes 3:10), why he prays that their hearts may be strengthened (1 Thes 3:13; 2 Thes 2:17; 3:3-5).

Sanctification

But the major aspect under which Paul presents the development of the Christian life of this community awaiting the Parousia is a process of *sanctification*. Paul has quite clearly taken over and spiritualized the cultic language of the Old Testament. God is holy and the place of his dwelling is holy, the place of his manifestation and self-revelation is holy, whether this be Mount Sinai (Ex 3:1,5) or its later counterpart the temple of Mount Zion (Ps 2:6; 50:2; 68:17f). Those worthy of appearing with the Lord in his final glory are "saints" (1 Thes 3:13), and this eschatological view of the term "saints" should never be lost from view, even when it is applied to the Church in its earthly condition. For the Church is basically the eschatological community which is preparing to meet the Lord in glory. Consequently, the whole process of the Christian life from beginning to end can be summed up as a process of *sanctification*. It always connotes a process of preparation for entering the divine presence, which the coming of Jesus will introduce in a consummate way (1 Thes 3:13): "blameless in holiness in the presence of our God and Father at the coming of our Lord Jesus with all his holy ones" (see also 5:23).

The process of sanctification involves simultaneously two elements: on the one hand, there is a clearly identifiable moral code with which Christianity is identified:

> You know the instructions we have given you in the Lord Jesus. It is God's will that you grow in holiness; that you abstain from immorality, each of you guarding his member in sanctity and honor, not in passionate desire as do the gentiles, who know not God; and that each refrain from overreaching or cheating his brother in the matter at hand, for the Lord is an avenger of such

things, as we once indicated to you by our testimony. God has not called us to immorality but to holiness; hence whoever rejects these instructions rejects not man but God who sends his Holy Spirit upon you (1 Thes 4:2-8 NAB).

There are some obscurities about parts of this text, due in part, no doubt, to the fact that Paul is simply recalling previous ethical instructions given to the Thessalonians. The phrase translated above, "Each of you guarding his member in sanctity and honor," may refer to sexual morality in general or the more specific practice of marrying an heiress despite impediments arising from kinship, in which case the translation would rather be, as in the RSV, "that each one of you know how to take a wife for himself in holiness and honor," and then "the matter in hand" of vs. 6 would refer to this specific problem. Otherwise, "the matter in hand" might mean a business matter or even adultery. In any case it is obvious that there are clear moral expectations for the Christian. He is not expected to be abandoned simply to unguided good intentions. He is given specific instructions behind which stands the authority of God himself.

But Paul is also aware that the process of sanctification is in the first place God's work. He it is who calls to holiness in the first place (1 Thes 2:12) and who alone can make those he calls worthy of his call (2 Thes 1:11). The process is stated most clearly in 1 Thes 5:23f: "May God, the author of peace, make you holy through and through. And may your whole being, spirit, soul and body be kept irreproachable for the coming of our Lord Jesus Christ. He who calls us is trustworthy, therefore he will do it."

The Holy Spirit

But the divine authorship is stressed most effectively by the fact that the process of sanctification is attributed to the

Holy Spirit: "But we are bound to give thanks to God always for you, brethren beloved by the Lord, because God chose you from the beginning to be saved through sanctification by the Spirit and belief in the truth" (2 Thes 2:13). Technically, the translation could also be rendered, "to be saved through sanctification of the spirit," meaning by spirit here the higher part of the soul. However, elsewhere when Paul speaks of sanctification he does not limit it to spirit but extends it to body and soul as well (1 Thes 5:23). Moreover Paul habitually attributes the work of sanctification to the Holy Spirit, and the omission of "Holy" before "Spirit" is understandable to avoid repeating a form of the word *hagios* already used. The best meaning, then, is that the process of salvation can be ascribed to two elements: the "truth" which is the content of the Christian revelation received in faith, and the "sanctification by the Spirit" which is the inward effect of God's action paralleling and corresponding to the outward content of the message appropriated by faith.

Even clearer is Paul's conclusion to his strong moral exhortation about holiness in 1 Thes 4:1-8. After saying strongly "For God has not called us to uncleanness but to holiness," (vs. 7), he adds, "Therefore whoever disregards this disregards not man but God, *who is giving his Holy Spirit to you*." Paul has just related the content of the Christian ethic. He claims divine authority by evoking the authority of God, whom the pagans manifest that they do not "know" because of their sexual license (4:5). But then by adding "who is giving his Holy Spirit to you" Paul moves away from the motive of divine authority to that of divine love and gift. He quotes implicitly Ez 37:14 and 36:27, in which the Lord promised to give his Spirit to his people so that they might observe his covenant and thus "know him." Though there is no suggestion of the justification conflict which will come later, it is clear that the motive which appeals most to Paul is the gift of God, which the sinner or the Christian back-slider rejects. Note that the verb "to give" is in the present tense, which indicates that God has not simply given the gift as a past act but is constantly in the process of giving the Spirit to the Church. Thus the Holy Spirit is not like a gift detached from the giver, wrapped and left at the doorstep of the receiver, but rather like the gift of a perpetual embrace or kiss in which the receiver experiences the real presence and touch of the Giver in person. Thus to reject this gift is not like discarding a worn-out gift received years ago but like pushing aside a present handshake or embrace. It is a rejection of the Giver in the action of giving.

Faith, Love, Hope

But sanctification is the fruit of love. This might have already been expected from the fact that Jesus taught that love is the supreme commandment, shaping all the rest (Mt 22: 34-40). It is explicitly stated by Paul in 1 Thes 3:12,13 that love is the agent which strengthens Christians and makes them blameless in holiness in the presence of God at the coming of Jesus. We may rightly expand this consideration to include faith and hope, always so closely related to love (1 Thes 1:3; 5:8; 1 Cor 13:13). As a matter of fact in 1 Thes 5:8 these three virtues are considered the armor of Christians who are "day people," living in the light and preparing for the Day of Christ. Paul will later say that these three attitudes are the characteristic of the present life and are its most abiding values (1 Cor 13:13), and there love comes as the climactic member of the triad because Paul is trying to call the Corinthians to a revival of love as the central dynamic for the exercise of the charismatic gifts. Here in Thessalonians, however, the three attitudes have a strong eschatological tone, an orientation toward the Lord's Second Coming, and this leads Paul to put the "hope of salvation" in the final place, because even faith and love are considered as preparations for the consummation on the Lord's day.

The same order appears at the very beginning of 1 Thes in a text whose density makes adequate translation a challenge: "We keep thanking God for all of you as we remember you in our prayers, ever aware how active your faith is, how dedicated your love and how persevering your hope in our Lord Jesus Christ, in the presence of our God and Father" (1 Thes 1:2,3). Of the three attitudes hope comes last and to it alone is joined the object "our Lord Jesus Christ." However, it is possible that Paul means this object of "faith" and "love" which otherwise would stand alone. If this is so, then the Lord Jesus Christ is the object of the Christians' faith as well as their love, a view which certainly agrees with Paul's statements elsewhere. However, the climactic stress certainly falls upon hope, and the addition of "before our God and Father," which some translators transfer earlier in the verse to modify the Greek *mnemoneuontes,* with the sense, "We constantly are mindful before our God and Father" (NAB), simply is a statement that the coming of Jesus in glory on his day will also inseparably mean a bringing of all Christian believers before the presence of God the Father (1 Thes 3:13). Thus the object of hope is not Jesus or God in general but specifically the coming of the Lord Jesus in glory and the entrance into the presence of God the Father.

The Greek of vs. 3, which we have tried to render in acceptable modern English style, literally reads, "The work of your faith and the labor of (your) love and the perseverance of (your) hope in our Lord. . . ." Each of these "virtues" has an outward manifestation by which its vitality can be judged. The Thessalonians' hope is manifested by their constancy under trial. The Greek *hypomone,* though sometimes translated "patience," has the strong sense of perseverance or constancy in the midst of persecution or trial. Such is precisely the concrete situation of the Thessalonians, and Paul finds admirable their loyalty and perseverance, which shows how strong is their hope in the Lord's Second Coming. Similarly, the vitality of their faith has been witnessed by its activity or "work." It has not been a lifeless faith but an energetic one, visible by its effects (2 Thes 1:11). (This text should not be forgotten when in Paul's later polemic he opposes faith to works. Both here and in Galatians 5:6 it is clear that when Paul speaks of faith he always means a living faith visible in works of love.)

The Thessalonians' charity has also become visible through their *toil*. Sometimes translated "labor," *kopos* means the kind of work that is long and heavy. Just as God's love becomes known in the total self-gift of Jesus (Gal 2:20; Rom 8:39), so the authenticity of Christian charity can be judged by its willingness to undertake the most burdensome tasks for the neighbor. We are not sure to what specific deeds Paul is referring here, but he considers the fraternal love of the Thessalonians so outstanding that only God himself could have taught them in the matter (1 Thes 4:9-10). It is possible, however, that just as the preceding text was followed with a reminder to "work with your hands as we directed you to do," (1 Thes 4:11), so here there may be a gentle admonition to those who have been idle. We learn from this that charity is not simply an emotion of affection or feeble wishful thinking but an energetic and active force that does not grow weary in doing good (2 Thes 3:13; 2:17). In the context of waiting for the Lord's coming, it is as if Paul were saying, "Don't just stand there, do something!"

What resources do the Thessalonians have to call upon to achieve the growth in strength, sanctification, faith, hope and love which Paul calls them to (1 Thes 4:10)? There is the final glory of reunion with Christ which is a certainty

(1 Thes 4:13-18; 5:9; 2 Thes 2:14) and the total triumph over evil which the final event will assure (2 Thes 1:5-10). There is, secondly, the fact of the divine election and call, which could not possibly be fruitless (1 Thes 1:4; 2 Thes 2:13), since God's fidelity is as present as his call (1 Thes 5:24). God's own word is the content of the message which they have heard, and it continues to work actively, almost as if it were an independent agent, among those who believe (1 Thes 2:13). The reason for this energy is that the word of God is not mere words but a message of power and the work of the Holy Spirit which gives the word its amazing fecundity (1 Thes 1:4,6).

God's Love

Behind the mystery of God's saving plan is the mystery of his graciousness (2 Thes 1:12) and his love. So pervasive is Paul's awareness of God's love for the Thessalonians that he can simply call them as if by a title, "the beloved of God" (1 Thes 1:4; 2 Thes 2:13). In 2 Thes 2:16,17 the intimate connection between God's love already manifested in the past and the consolation and strength which the Thessalonians need in the present is clearly emphasized: "May our Lord Jesus Christ himself and God our Father, who loved us and gave us a consolation that is everlasting and a hope that is precious in its graciousness, console your hearts and strengthen them in every good work and word."

Several things are noteworthy about this text: (1) The Lord Jesus is named here before the Father, which surely indicates an equality with him in the bestowal of the favor Paul prays for; (2) The Greek words *autos* ("himself") and *agapesas* ("who loved") and the rest of the verbs are in the singular, although the subject is obviously plural — both the Lord Jesus and the Father; it is obvious that in the bestowal of grace Paul considers them one source operating together;

(3) The aorist tense of the verbs "loved" and "gave" refer to a specific past action situated in time and must therefore refer to the mystery of God's love shown in the self-gift of Jesus on the cross. It could also refer to the Holy Spirit who gives everlasting consolation by granting a foretaste of the glory to which Christians are called; (4) Paul asks that this mystery of the God who loves without measure and consoles without end become a present reality touching the Thessalonians and strengthening them in action and in word; he asks, in other words, that they may know the encouragement of experiencing the closeness of God's love for them.

A similar thought appears in 2 Thes 3:5, which admits of several translations. The most literal one is, "May the Lord lead your hearts into the love of God and the patience of Christ." The question here is whether the genitives following "love" and "patience" are objective, in which case the sense would be, "May the Lord lead you to love God and endure for Christ," or whether they are subjective, and then the sense would be, "May the Lord direct your hearts into the love that God has for you and the endurance which Christ has shown." In the light of the overall teaching of the letters to the Thessalonians, the latter translation seems to be the better one. It is in contemplating and experiencing God's love for them that they will also be able to endure the persecutions and trials they are experiencing with the very endurance which Jesus showed in his passion, sustained as he was by the awareness of his Father's love. This interpretation is also suggested by 1 Thes 3:12: "May the Lord fill you up and make you overflow in love for one another and toward all . . ." The "all" surely is meant to include not only strangers outside the community but also the persecutors. To love these was taught by Jesus' word and example.

Already from these two earliest letters our search for Paul's teaching on the spiritual life has yielded precious first-fruits. The Christian life is basically a life lived in a community of believers who await eagerly and long for the manifestation of Jesus their Lord in glory and who in the meantime dedicate themselves to loving one another and all men. To grow in this love, which is simply a response to the Father's own love manifested in Jesus Christ, is basically to be sanctified and thus to be worthy of the Father's presence into which the returning Lord Jesus will introduce his "holy ones."

Chapter Three

WHAT MEAN THESE CHAINS?

Suggested readings: Acts 18:18-19:40;
The Letter to the Philippians

WITHIN two years after writing the letters to the Thessalonians Paul undertook his third missionary journey which brought him to Ephesus (Acts 18:13-19:40). Here he began a ministry that lasted for almost three years, perhaps the most successful period of Paul's career. According to the picture Luke draws for us, Paul's success in the city was so great that he became a threat to the pagan image-making trade, and the silversmith Demetrius could exclaim that the new religion had spread "almost over the whole province of Asia" (Acts 19:26). Paul himself would write from Ephesus "that here a door has been opened to me, great and evident" (1 Cor 16:9). With the help of his companions Timothy, Erastus, Gaius, Aristarchus, and Epaphras (Act 19:22, 29; Col 1:7), Christian communities were founded in Colossae, Laodicea, Hierapolis (Col 1:7; 2:1; 4:12f.), Troas (2 Cor 2:12; Acts 20:5-12) and most probably the other communities in Asia mentioned in Revelations 1:11: Smyrna, Pergamum, Thyatira, Sardis, and Philadelphia.

But the Ephesus experience was also one of danger and persecution (Acts 20:19; 21:27). For the first time in his life Paul could admit that at one point in the Ephesian ministry he was "crushed beyond measure — beyond our strength, so that we were weary even of life" (2 Cor 1:8) and was in serious danger of death (2 Cor 1:9f.; 11:23,26). Although the Acts are silent about this matter, it is likely that the distress involved imprisonment. This Ephesian imprisonment would provide the ideal setting for the epistle to the Philippians. While some scholars still hold to the Roman origin of the letter, many reasons make its Ephesian origin more probable. For one thing, such an origin would fit the chronology of Acts and Corinthians perfectly. The many comings and goings which the letter supposes between the Philippians and the imprisoned Paul would require an extremely long time if he were in Rome, whereas they could easily be made in the seven day journey that separated Philippi from Ephesus. The fact that the Philippians and Paul assume (4:10) that they had no occasion to help him since his first visit would be hard to explain if Paul were in Rome, for by that time he had visited them twice on his third missionary journey, whereas at the Ephesus date he had not returned even once. Finally, the references to the Praetorian guard (1:13) and the house of Caesar (4:22), which many commentators had taken as sure proofs of the Roman origin of the letter, are now known to fit equally well the situation in Ephesus, where there was a detachment of the Praetorian Guard and where persons belonging to the "household of Caesar" managed the imperial bank in Asia.

Compassion and Joy

Where is Paul now in his own spiritual development? He had known the shadow of prison bars and the weight of chains before — at Philippi precisely. But that had been brief and his deliverance miraculous (Acts 16:16-40). Now the chains weigh heavily (1:7,13,14,17). Accustomed to prodigious activity and movement, he is now forced into solitude and reflection. Accustomed to spending himself in preaching and teaching, he has now had to learn how to receive. Not that this was the first time Paul had received financial support from them. Although quite poor (2 Cor 8:2), the Philippians had sent him aid at Thessalonica (Phil 4:16), and again at Corinth (2 Cor 11:9), and it was the Philippians who first responded to Paul's collection for the poor in Jerusalem (2 Cor 8:2; Phil 4:15). But now there was a particularly warm touch to their help, sent to him through Epaphroditus (4:18), and Paul lets the warmth of his feeling vibrate through the letter. Recalling how much the Philippians have shared in his work then and now (1:5, 7), he tells them that he has them in his heart and loves them and longs for them with the tender affection of Christ Jesus (1:7,8; 4:2). The Greek expression in 1:8 means literally "in the bowels of Christ Jesus." It evokes the Hebrew *rahamim* which the Old Testament used for the tenderness and compassion that a mother has for her child. The expression was used repeatedly to stress the tenderness of God's mercy and love for His people. The synoptics use the verb form to describe the ease with which Jesus is moved by compassion for human need (Matt 9:36; 14:14; 15:32; 20:34) and the similar vulnerability which Jesus expects his disciples to have (Lk 10:33). In Paul's case, however, it is the Philippians' response to his needs that evokes this tenderness of affection for them. Paul's warmth and sensitivity appear again in his feelings about Epaphroditus: "Indeed he was ill and near to death. But God had mercy on him, and not only on him, but on me also, lest I should have sorrow upon sorrow. I am the more eager to send him, therefore, that you might rejoice at seeing him again, and that I may be less anxious" (2:27).

But the feeling that predominates in the entire epistle is that of joy. In fact, if any of Paul's letters could be called "the letter of joy," it is the epistle to the Philippians. The references to joy and rejoicing are abundant: (1:4,25; 2:2, 17f.,28f.; 4:1,10). The major source of Paul's joy is the vitality of the Philippian community itself. They are his joy and crown (4:1; cf. 1 Thes 2:19). If the Thessalonians were remarkable for the joy with which they received the good news in the first place (1 Thes 1:6), Paul can equate the Philippians' progress in faith with their progress in joy (1: 25). Paul's experience is preparing him for the day in which he will describe joy as the first fruit of the Spirit after love (Gal 5:22).

Some of the elements of Paul's letter to the Philippians will not surprise us. His conviction of the coming Parousia is still strong (3:20), he sees salvation as a future event involving the bodily resurrection of the just (3:21), and the condition of this community which awaits the Parousia is one of discontinuity with the world — although Paul now believes more positively that the Church can be an inspiration to it (2:15). The present Christian life is one that is subject to a law of constant progress (1:25; 3:12-16), a theme we have already met in Thessalonians (1 Thes 4:1,10; 3:11-13). That it is ultimately God's work appears from 2:12f.: "Work out your own salvation with fear and trembling, for God is working in you both to will and to accomplish in fulfillment of His benevolent purpose." In the history of Christian thought, the last portion of this text has sometimes been translated "as he pleases," and the entire text used to generate an anxiety about personal salvation. But this interpretation goes counter to Paul's overall theology and the intention of this particular text. The "fear and trembling" means a religious reverence and awe that could not possibly be engendered by an anxiety about either God's intentions or the outcome. Rather the "fear and trembling" is the realization that Christian response is precisely co-operation in a divine work, a holy project initiated and guided by God's loving purpose. A further indication that their growth is God's work is the prayer of 1:9-11, which strongly resembles 1 Thes 3:11-13 but differs from it sufficiently to be examined separately below.

Unanimity

Let us now turn to elements of newness that we see emerging in this epistle. For one thing, the community of the Philippians seems more highly structured than anything we have met thus far. While in 1 Thes there was a reference to "those who labor among you and are over you in the Lord and admonish you" (1 Thes 5:12), here we meet for the first time *bishops* and *deacons,* who are carefully noted in the address (1:1).

Another new element is the concern for unanimity. Like the Thessalonians, the Philippians are invited to walk worthily of their call, but whereas the former were simply encouraged to continue to grow in love for one another, the latter are urged to aim at a unity of mind (1:27; 2:1-5). Is this new concern due to the fact that personality conflicts have begun to appear in the community? Two devoted women in the community, Evodia and Syntyche, were at odds about something (4:2f.) and that minor spat may have been all there was to Paul's concern about unity — Paul discretely waiting to the end of the letter to mention their names, and that in a very supportive way (vs. 3).

But it is equally possible that Paul, now having experienced more serious brushes with false teaching, has moved beyond the simple exhortation to grow in charity and has become preoccupied with the doctrinal shape of the Christian faith and the need within every Christian community to be at one about it. In any case we can at least say that the debate about justification, entirely absent from the letters to the Thessalonians, has begun to rear its head. While it is not as violent as it will become in Galatians and Romans and does not appear to be the danger it will be seen to be there, there is the warning to avoid the "cutters," the promoters of circumcision (3:1ff.), and this introduces the long passage, already discussed, in which Paul contrasts his present status as a Christian with his previous advantages as a Jew and Pharisee (3:4-16). From this passage may be retained, for future reference, the fact that justification by the law is equated with "my own justification," which is opposed to justification in faith in Jesus Christ (3:9). The danger, however, does not seem to be great in the Philippian community, and Paul is happy to dispatch the earthly concerns of the Judaizers (food and circumcision, 3:19) with an allusion to the cross of Christ which points to the love and gift of God (3:18) and an evoking of the glorious destiny of bodily resurrection which awaits all in Christ (3:21).

Knowledge and Discernment

However, the emerging concern for light as well as ardor in the Christian life appears in the prayer which early in the letter Paul offers for his readers: "And this is the object of my prayer, that your love abound more and more in knowledge and all discernment, that you may distinguish true values, that you may be pure and blameless for the day of Christ, filled with the fruit of righteousness that comes from Jesus Christ, for the glory and praise of God" (Phil 1:9-11).

The structure of this prayer closely resembles 1 Thes 3:11-13. In both cases Paul expresses his desire that the charity of his readers grow. Whereas in the Thessalonian letter he prays simply that their charity abound and overflow toward one another and to all men, in the Philippian letter he specifies the area of the desired growth as "knowledge and all discernment."

The word used for knowledge here is not the more general

gnosis which, when followed by a complement, as for example in the expression "the knowledge of God," can leave the reader in doubt as to whether the expression means God's own knowledge or a knowledge about God. The Greek word used here is *epignosis,* which always refers to the knowledge of an object, and in most cases directs the knower's attention to some particular aspect of the object or person known. That is why the verb form is often translated "recognize." Ulysses on preparing to return in disguise to his father's house wonders whether his father will "recognize" him, that is discern and identify in the object seen, in this case a beggar standing before him, his own son. Similarly, Rhoda upon answering the door, recognized the person of Peter by his voice (Act 12:14). The word is thus eminently suited for the kind of knowledge which Paul desires for his community. It will be a clearer, more profound knowledge of the object of their faith, namely Jesus Christ and all the riches contained in him (Col 2:3). It will also be a kind of "value knowledge," inasmuch as, experiencing more deeply who Jesus is, they may more readily choose him over the other values clamoring for their loyalty — specifically in the case of the Philippians, the propaganda of the Judaizers.

If Paul sees the need for some teaching on this matter, which he does later on in the epistle, he sees this knowledge here as proceeding not from teaching but rather from a more fervent love. Love, born of the truth of God's revelation, seeks first to know more purely the truth of which it has been born. Thus we see Paul coming to a realization of something that was not so clear in the letter to the Thessalonians. There the only function of charity seemed to be its labor (1 Thes 1:3) or its pouring out of itself in generosity to others in the community or outside (1 Thes 3:12). Here, however, charity has a clearly contemplative function, which Paul considers to be the first area in which charity should grow. Has he learned that without a concern to develop its contemplative dimension, the very fervor of its activity is likely to grow cold? We can only guess that such is the case.

Closely associated with the growth in knowledge is the growth in discernment. The Greek word here is *aisthesis*. It is an old Greek word used in classical times as a hunting term for the track or the scent. A dog's ability to "discern" which way to turn in pursuit of game is a marvel to hunters even today. The word was also used for the ability of merchants to tell cloth of precious value, just as a connoisseur can distinguish excellent wine from cheap. As a boy I remember watching with amazement a mohair sorter in my father's warehouse take a fleece of hair, detach a handful of it and merely by his touch make a rapid and certain judgment as to which of about thirty categories the handful belonged to, and cast it into the appropriate box. A judgment of the hair's quality, its length, smoothness, and even its width, was made by a split-second touch.

That, I would learn years later in my biblical studies, is *aisthesis*. Paul applies it here in the moral sense for the quick and intuitive judgments which the Christian must make in the midst of the many options which face him daily. This is suggested by the sequence which says literally "that you may distinguish the things that differ," and may be otherwise rendered, "that you may approve true values," or "that you may approve the better things," or simply "that you may make the right decisions." This ability Paul sees as necessary in order to bring Christians in purity and holiness to the day of Christ, the day of His final coming. Paul has become even more aware now than he was in the letters to the Thessalonians that the Church which awaits the day of the Lord is also the Church immersed in daily living in a world which presents a spectrum of values, some of which are good and upright enough to be pursued by Christians (4:8) and others which must be condemned and fled (3:2, 18).

Thus we begin to see Paul taking more seriously the meaning of the present development of the Christian life. It is not merely a question of persevering in hope and fidelity to the end when the Lord comes but of knowing how to make Christian sense of life in the world right now. The Christ whom we await can also somehow be found in the interim. Paul seems to have been brought to this view by a meditation on his own sufferings and brush with death. To this we will devote our final and central consideration about the epistle to the Philippians.

Death and Resurrection Now

From the epistles to the Thessalonians we recall how the Parousia was the central focus of Paul's teaching and spiritual energy and how the Resurrection of Christ the Lord was understood to be a forecast and guarantee of the final day. The cross of Jesus is never mentioned, the sufferings of Jesus are only indirectly alluded to (1 Thes 1:6; 2 Thes 3:5), and the death of Jesus even less clearly alluded to. In 1 Thes 4:14 the Christian dead are described as "those who have fallen asleep through Jesus." Though the expression is sometimes translated, "have died believing in Jesus," justice must be done to the Greek preposition *dia,* which does not mean *in* but *through.* The dense meaning of this cryptic phrase seems to be that Jesus is the cause of the death of Christians — not in the sense that he brings about their physical death but in the sense that he is the author of *Christian death,* since in virtue of his own death and Resurrection he has changed the entire meaning of death itself. It is no longer a falling asleep in relation to a previous state of wakefulness but a falling asleep with the assurance of the future awakening at the Resurrection. All of this is, however, very un-

developed, and the thought of Jesus' own death hardly seems
to have a theological importance at all in Thessalonians.

In Philippians the new importance Paul sees in the mystery
of suffering and death appears in four ways. First and most
obviously there is the long passage in Philippians 2:1-11.
Exhorting the Philippians to self-effacement for the sake of
their brothers and sisters in the Lord, Paul introduces a hymn
about Christ who set aside glory to become a servant to the
point of death on a cross and who was therefore exalted in
glory to God's right hand (Phil 2:6-11). It is a commonplace
among biblical scholars today to point out that here Paul
has simply borrowed a hymn from the liturgy of some early
Christian community, most probably a Palestinian one, which
has taken the Old Testament motif of the Suffering Servant
of Isaiah 52-53 and applied it to the stages of Jesus' incar-
nation, death and exaltation. The hymn, we should note,
says nothing about the redemptive value of this magnificent
act on the part of Jesus but is concerned rather with the
rhythm of humiliation and abasement which wins God's
response of exalting his Servant to glory. As such, Jesus is
simply presented to the Christian as a model for self-effacement. We have yet to encounter the deep sense of mystical
union with the suffering Lord and the redemptive value of
Christian suffering.

Paul's Own Death

But the movement in that deeper and mystical direction
begins to appear in the new understanding of death which
we see Paul clearly affirming as he contemplates the possibility of his own imminent death in 1:23. This is a second
level of Paul's theology of death which appears in Philippians. Whereas he had been completely silent in 1 Thes 5
about the present state of the Christian dead, he clearly
affirms that if his imprisonment leads to his death, this will

mean immediate union with Christ, a lot he ardently longs for: "I long to be freed of this life and to be with Christ."

The Fellowship of his Sufferings

But he is equally aware that he may not soon die and if he is to remain it is certainly reasonable to project, on tho basis of his missionary experience to this point, that much of his life will be marked by suffering. Is this suffering simply a hanging on in hope until the Lord comes, or has Paul now begun to see a new meaning in his suffering? In 3:10 he defines his ambition, as we might expect, in terms of knowing Jesus Christ (in contrast to his previous ambition of knowing the law). This is not surprising nor is it new. But the phrases he immediately adds to develop what "knowing Christ" involves give us a glimpse of Paul's deepening insight: "to know him and the power of his resurrection and the fellowship of his sufferings." Another way of translating the phrase is: "to know Christ and what a power his Resurrection is and what it is to share his sufferings."

Does Paul mean by "knowing the power of Christ's Resurrection" simply knowing in faith that Paul will one day rise from the dead? This is suggested by the sequence in vs. 11, "that if possible I may attain to the Resurrection from the dead." However, if that is all that Paul means here, he would be guilty of severe redundance, and moreover the parallelism with the following expression "the fellowship of his sufferings" surely means to describe a present experience — the word "know" also obviously indicates an experiential knowledge. The "power of his resurrection" is therefore the power presently experienced in Paul's life, not only the power to preach with boldness (1 Thes 1:5; 2 Cor 3:12; Eph 6:19) and miracles and wonders worked in the name of Jesus (Rom 15:19) but also the power to undertake the heaviest labors and endure the most severe persecutions, including imprisonment.

Thus the power of his Resurrection is closely associated now with the fellowship of his sufferings, and the latter means a "growing conformed to his death." The death of Jesus has now become for Paul a mystery into which he has entered by accepting the person of Christ into his life. The Greek *symmorphizomemos* is a word of Paul's own coining. It means to express both an outward likeness in the suffering as well as an inward communion with Christ in his death.

It is not specifically Paul's *death* but his *sufferings* which reproduce the pattern of Christ's death. Thus, as he will later say to the Corinthians, "death is at work in us but life in you" (2 Cor 4:12). Here Paul is thinking of his own sufferings as the means with which he communes with the person of Jesus Christ. Later in Rom 6: 4,5 he will describe baptism in terms of being buried with or grafted on to Christ. That later sacramental development seems to be made possible by his own experiencing of the mystery of Christ's death through apostolic sufferings — the third level of Paul's death-theology in Philippians.

Intercessory Value

There is a fourth new value he now sees in these apostolic sufferings. Not only are they united with the suffering of Jesus, but they are endowed with an intercessory value. "Even if I am to be poured out as a libation on the sacrificial offering of your faith . . ." (2:17). Paul had previously in 1:23,24 considered his imminent death as a going to the Lord and the possibility of his staying as an opportunity to work at promoting the faith of the Philippians. Now he sees that his death itself could be more than a simple separation from the Philippians and a reunion with the Lord. It could be — in fact he sees that it *would be* — a sacrifice bringing special divine blessing to the faith of the community. His sufferings and possible death therefore have an intercessory value. They are redemptive and life-bringing for his very mission (cf. 2 Cor 4:12).

We may conclude that Paul's suffering and his brush with death in Ephesus, the chains which he bears, have brought him much deeper insight into his own mission. Paul is called not simply to be the announcer of the end, the coming day of the Lord, but to be a vessel who embodies the mystery of Christ's death and Resurrection which he preaches. His chains have brought him a communion with Jesus quite beyond anything he might have expected on the road to Damascus. If it is a communing with the sufferings and death of Jesus, it is also a mission of great joy and an experience of the power which this communion gives him. In fact, he can say that even in his chains, "There is no limit to what I can do through him who strengthens me" (4:15).

Chapter Four

THE SPIRIT AND THE BODY

Suggested readings: 1 and 2 Corinthians.

THE period we are discussing is the one of Paul's most prodigious literary activity. Between his arrival in Ephesus and his departure from Corinth on the third missionary journey Paul carried on a correspondence which has come down to us today in the two letters to the Corinthians and the letters to the Galatians and Romans. So important are these letters in understanding the thought of Paul that some authors (mistakenly) discount all his other writings in determining Paul's genuine thought. However extreme this view, it is nevertheless true that in these letters Paul develops his teaching with a depth that matches the breadth of subject matter which he undertakes. Since the letters were written in such close proximity it will not be easy to determine major developments from one to the other, and we are on a better track by considering all of them together as witnesses to Paul's development at this period of his life. Consequently, while we will try to discern what is the major spiritual theme of each letter in order, we will feel quite free, as we monitor emergent themes, to listen to the other voices in this quartet.

From Ephesus Paul carried on a vigorous correspondence with the Corinthians. The two letters which bear this name presently in our collection of Paul's letters are only what has survived. In 1 Cor 5:9 Paul informs us of a previous letter

51

he had written to the Corinthians (we can call it letter A). It was a warning to baptized Christians who were falling back into pagan practices. Seemingly the letter produced its desired effect but it also raised many questions concerning Paul's meaning, and thus the community addressed an official letter to Paul, probably sending it by a delegation of three leaders of the community, Stephanas, Fortunatus and Achaicus (1 Cor 16:15ff.). In addition to the list of "cases of conscience" which were presented to Paul, other reports had reached him amplifying the picture of the Corinthian crisis. The community was divided into various factions: one group promoting a return to pagan moral standards by appealing to the new gnosis and liberty of the gospel; a group of ascetics in reaction to the libertines, some Christians suing their brother-Christians before pagan courts of law; but especially a division and rivalry over the personalities of different apostles or preachers who had visited the community. This spirit of division had even entered the common worship, so that the Lord's supper became a scene of various groups eating apart. And in the midst of this, enthusiastic individualism was ruling the Christian assembly to such an extent that the use of the charisms (tongues, interpretation, and prophecy) was becoming a source of scandal to gentile visitors. Thus Paul writes to correct this situation, and this letter (Letter B) is our canonical "First Corinthians."

Concerning the canonical Second Corinthians we join those scholars who consider it a later anthology of various letters written to Corinth concerning Paul's mission and authority and the collection to be made for the poor in Jerusalem. Thus, if we consider Letter A to be the first of Paul's letters to the Corinthians and Letter B our present First Corinthians, then Letter C would be Paul's conciliatory defense of his apostolate (2 Cor 2:14-7:4), Letter D a vigorous, polemical defense of his apostolate (2 Cor 10:1-13:14),

Letter E the celebration of reconciliation with the Corinthians (2 Cor 1:1-2:13; 7:5-16), Letter F Paul's recommendation of Titus and the collection (2 Cor 8:1-24), and finally Letter G, Paul's final word on the collection (9:1-27).

The complete Corinthian correspondence, then, is a mine which we may expect to yield precious ore in our inquiry into Paul's own spiritual development as he responds to the many-faceted crisis. Attempts to synthesize growth themes may be pretentious, but it does appear that Paul's understanding of the Christian life at this point can be understood under the relationship of the Spirit to the Body.

The Spirit

The word *spirit* as we have already observed, is used by Paul to describe man's outreach to transcendence, his openness to encounter God and be moved by him (1 Cor 2:6-13; Rom 8:15) or it is used for the Spirit of God himself, the Holy Spirit. For Paul the Spirit is the distinguishing factor of the gospel over against the regime of law under which the Jews lived prior to their becoming Christians (Gal 3:2). And this difference appeared from the very moment of their becoming Christians — it is confirmation of the word (1 Thes 1:5; 1 Cor 1:6; Rom 15:18f.). The Holy Spirit means not only a new experience of God as *Abba* (Gal 4:6; Rom 8:15), not only the source of a new moral life (Gal 5:25), but just as the Word of God continues to work in the believing community (1 Thes 2:13) so the Holy Spirit continues to manifest his presence through various gifts (1 Cor 1:7). To these early Christians the Holy Spirit appears less as an object of faith than as a motive of faith. The Spirit is known as an incredible power released within the community by reason of its attachment to Jesus Christ.

The church of Corinth was no exception to this universal experience. From the letters it even seems that Corinth was

the primary laboratory for evolving a theology of the Holy
Spirit. The Spirit manifested his presence in the community
through various surprising gifts, particularly those of tongues,
prophecies and knowledge. Although Paul will have much to
say about the *use* of these gifts, he praises God for their
existence in the Corinthian community (1 Cor 1:4-7), he
says that he can thank God that he speaks in tongues more
abundantly than any of his readers (1 Cor 14:18), and he
especially recommends prophecy because it so clearly builds
up the community (1 Cor 14:1-5). He can, in fact, urge the
Corinthians to seek earnestly after the gifts (14:1). Paul is
also quite convinced that only the Holy Spirit can reveal
God's secret wisdom (1 Cor 2:9-16). The Holy Spirit is
indeed the "down payment" of the glory of the resurrection
to come (2 Cor 1:22; 5:5) inasmuch as he gives a foretaste
of the final consummation. So convinced is Paul that the
Spirit is the principle of the fulness of life that in Galatians
he will make the utterly astounding statement (for a Jew!)
that the Holy Spirit is the fulfillment of the promise made to
Abraham (Gal 3:14). It follows from this that the Holy
Spirit is identified with the Christian life itself and that
growth in this life will be a matter of following the impulse
of the Spirit. In all of this Paul and the Corinthians are
agreed.

Misunderstandings

But there are some elements about the Corinthians' understanding of the Spirit which are disturbing to Paul, and
he sets out to correct them. Under heavy Hellenistic influence the Corinthian community did not escape the contemporary Greek infatuation with "gnosis," knowledge particularly in the sense of esoteric knowledge of "mysteries," such
as it was understood in the mystery religions, one of whose
major centers, Eleusis, was but a few miles from Corinth.

While not the full-blown gnosticism of the second century, the gnosticizing tendency at Corinth already reflected the desire to cut any tethering cord to earthly, "somatic" existence and to float free like a balloon into the unscaled heights of "mystery knowledge." Such pursuit of knowledge so severed the unity of body and spirit that it fostered illuministic individualism as the real interest of man's psychic energies. As for man's somatic relationships (his own body, his social relationships and his relation to the material world) these were irrelevant to spiritual progress, and thus what one did "in the body" did not really matter. Such a rationale provided a very comfortable framework for maintaining the pagan chasm between religion and morality, between "spirituality" and "ethics."

Thus, for example, in relation to the individual's body, fornication, considered a perfectly normal practice in paganism, could be continued in Christianity since the gift of the Spirit freed the Christian from any scruples about the flesh and focused his spirit solely on the knowledge of mysteries and, perhaps for Jewish enthusiasts, on "signs of power." Since the aim of such spirituality was the individual's conquest of mystery, he was also freed from any sense of responsibility to the community, for the "other" could be, at most, a competitive challenge to one's own advance in "knowledge." Finally, a past historical event such as the death and Resurrection of Jesus of Nazareth would not be something "eschatological" or ultimate, to which one submits in "obedience of faith" (Rom 1:5) but at most a symbol for the individual's journey to knowledge. Thus once one has interpreted it properly, one has mastered it and, by making it serve one's own spiritual advancement, now stands above it. In short, Corinthian gnosticism was an ego trip of the most subtle variety. It was an ego trip quite different from that of the legal observance Paul had pursued as a Pharisee. For that reason we find little of the polemic against the law which dominates Galatians and Romans. In fact, although Paul may have been waging that very polemic at the same time he wrote to the Corinthians, he deliberately avoids any condemnation of the law (except for 1 Cor 15: 56) because many of the Corinthians have, precisely, found a way of exempting themselves from any ethical expectations, and Paul certainly does not want to foster such an illusion. But to pursue individualistically the "knowledge of mysteries" is as much an ego trip as it was for Paul to pursue "knowledge of the law" when it is obvious God has a better idea for bringing man to the fullness of perfection.

This context helps us to understand the important refinements which Paul brings to the theology of the Spirit in his correspondence with the Corinthians. He roots the Christian experience of the Spirit to the event of Jesus (1 Cor 12:3). More specifically, Christian wisdom distinguishes itself from worldly wisdom (no matter how "spiritual" such wisdom might seem) by its foundation in the cross (1 Cor 1:17-2:9). Then, in his first discussion of the divine wisdom given by the Spirit, Paul says that "the Spirit we have received is not the spirit of the world but the Spirit from God, that we might understand the gifts bestowed on us by God" (1 Cor 2:12). The expression translated here "the gifts bestowed" is in the Greek the single word *charisthenta,* the aorist passive participle. It refers to God's gracious bestowal of his gifts as an historical act accomplished at a definite moment in time. Paul no doubt compacts into this expression the death and Resurrection of Jesus and the gift of the Spirit which became realities for the Corinthians at the moment of their conversion and baptism. Implicit is the suggestion that what the Spirit leads one to experience and know is not some elusive, unpredictable esoteric mystery but rather the saving event already accomplished in Jesus Christ.

The Body

Another way in which Paul reacts against the incipient gnosticism is by relating the Spirit to the *body*. By this term Paul does not mean "body" in the quite restricted sense in which we take it as the counterpart of the "soul." Nor, on the other hand, is the term *body* completely identical with the "flesh," though at times the terms are used interchangeably (1 Cor 6:16,17). Body really stands for the whole person from the viewpoint of his solidarity with the created universe (Rom 8:23) and especially his solidarity with his fellow human beings (Heb 13:3). While the body can become a body of sin (Rom 6:6), it can also be the body of the redemption (Rom 8:23). That is why Paul can speak even of a spiritual body (*soma pneumatikon,* 1 Cor 15:44), a concept very difficult for us who are prone to think of materiality and spirituality as incompatible opposites. Not so for Paul. Bodiliness suggests solidarity, interlocking relationship. And spirituality means docility to the Spirit. Thus whatever is touched and transformed into God's saving plan becomes spirit, even though it be material.

The Risen Body of the Lord

The inter-penetration of spirit and body appears most clearly in the case of the risen humanity of the Lord Jesus. The Holy Spirit (or "the Spirit of holiness") is the agent of Jesus' Resurrection from the dead and his enthronement *in power* as Son of God (Rom 1:4). Able to be crucified because he shared the weakness of humanity, he now lives because of the *power of God* (2 Cor 13:4), an expression that is equivalent to Spirit. The tradition related in Acts 2:32f. is that God the Father, having raised Jesus from the dead and exalted him to his right hand, gave him first the promised Holy Spirit, and Jesus in turn poured this out upon the Church.

But Paul associates the gift of the Spirit even more closely
to the risen humanity of Christ. Christ becomes a spiritual
body (1 Cor 15:44). How can this be? To explain it Paul
introduces the contrast between the first man, Adam, and
the last Adam, who is Christ. Quoting Gen 2:7, Paul says that
Adam as a result of God's creative act became a living being
(*psychen zosan*). The full context of Gen 2:7 is necessary
to understand Paul's meaning here: "The Lord God formed
man out of the clay of the ground and blew into his nostrils
the breath of life, and so man became a living being." One
will note the element of materiality in that Adam is from the
adamah, Earthman from earth; the element of the spirit in
the breath of life breathed into him by God; and the element
of natural or human vitality ("a living being") which results
from this gift. By his Resurrection from the dead Christ was
not simply returned to the natural life of Adam (resuscitation,
psychen zosan), but having received the living breath of the
Spirit from the Father in his humanity, that very humanity
is now "life-giving spirit." In this way Paul considers the
risen humanity of the new Adam to be the universal source
of life for the new creation. The Lord Jesus and the Spirit are
identified: "The Lord is the Spirit" (2 Cor 3:17,18). The
"spiritualization" of Jesus in the Resurrection happens in a
way which preserves intact his character as *body,* and it is
precisely this that makes possible his solidarity with each
Christian and the Church.

The Body of the Christian

And thus we are led to the second of the pillars of Paul's
body theology, the body of the individual Christian and its
relationship to Christ and the Spirit. Paul will not allow the
Corinthian enthusiasm to draw him away from his preferred
designation of the life of Christians on earth as a life "in the
body" (2 Cor 5:6,10). How crucial this is for Paul's pneuma-

tology becomes obvious from 1 Cor 6:15-20. Beginning in
v. 12 Paul quotes a principle which he himself had probably
given to the Corinthians in the matter of foods: "All things
are lawful for me." The Corinthians had gladly accepted this
declaration of independence and had applied it to sexuality
as well. Paul does not withdraw the principle but notes that
mere removal of an external prohibition is not sufficient to
determine what the Christian should or should not do. Freedom is a matter of not being enslaved by *anything,* whether
it be law or license. And since the new freedom derives
uniquely from one's belonging to the Lord, whatever would
hinder this union is an infringement of freedom. Paul sees
fornication precisely as a violation of the new freedom that
has been given the Christian by reason of his belonging to the
Lord. "The body . . . is for the Lord, and the Lord for the
body" (vs. 13). As we shall see later on, Paul's morality is
neither legalistic nor rational — it is "mystical." He views
this particular question uniquely from the viewpoint of the
destiny of the Christian's body which is to be raised by the
Lord's power and united with him in glory. He considers the
present purpose of Christ's glorified existence as being the
principle of resurrection for his members (vs. 14). And
then he adds, "Do you not know that your bodies are members of Christ?" (vs. 15). Quite clearly Paul conceives the
Christian life as a bodily union with the Lord. It is not possible for the Corinthian libertine to say that he gives his spirit
to the Lord and his body to the prostitute. To give one's
body to the prostitute is a form of spiritual adultery, since
one's body belongs to the Lord as much as one's spirit. Paul
then quotes Gen 2:24 to show how sexual union involves
becoming "one body" with the person to whom one is joined.
The implication is that he who is joined to the Lord becomes
one body with him, in fact even becomes a member of
Christ's body.

However, Paul goes on to say that he who is united to the Lord (and the Greek verb in vs. 17 is exactly the same as in vs. 16, suggesting a physical union) becomes more than one body with the Lord; he also becomes one *spirit* with him. This verse is not meant to deny the bodily union with Christ which has already been clearly expressed in vs. 15 but simply to show that the effect of this bodily union is, unlike prostitution, a spiritualization, since the Christ to whom one is joined is a *spiritual body* (1 Cor 15:44). This same point is made in 12:13: "In one Spirit we were all baptized into one body and we have all been given to drink of the same Spirit." The "one body" into which we have been baptized is not the corporate body of Christians of which we have become members but very starkly the body of the risen Lord Jesus. Baptism is a plunging *into* that unique body, a bodily union with him who is also spirit and consequently and inseparably it is a drinking of the Spirit who indwells and flows from that body. For, just as Christ is the spiritual body, he is also the spiritual rock (1 Cor 10:4).

This same pattern of thought appears ir the sequence of the text we have been examining concerning sexual morality: "Do you not know that your body is a temple of the Holy Spirit, who is in you, whom you have from God?" (1 Cor 6:19), so that one can say equivalently that the Christian's body is a member of Christ and a temple of the Holy Spirit. This is possible only because the body to which one is joined is itself the temple of the Holy Spirit, and the Christian simply benefits from the spiritual effect of his bodily union with this place of the Spirit's dwelling.

The result is that the Christian's body, having become the temple of God through the indwelling of the Spirit, is now, like the sanctuary of Jerusalem, the place where God reveals his glory and where he is worshipped. Just as one does not "see" the presence of God in the temple directly but knows it from what he sees in the physical arrangement of the building, the altar, the liturgy and all other sensible elements, so anyone who cares to see may know the presence of God through the somatic comportment of the Christian. Body and spirit are, according to Paul, absolutely inseparable: "So glorify God in your body" (vs, 20). It is exactly the same thought which appears in Rom 12:1: "Present your bodies as a living sacrifice, holy and acceptable to God, your spiritual worship." The bodily life of the Christian is a liv'ng liturgy.

Baptism, Eucharist

But this business of a physical union with the risen humanity of Jesus is difficult to visualize or imagine. How can the Christian who lives a very secular life claim to be physically or somatically united with the resurrected Jesus? Is it merely a matter of faith in him? Is it only a union in spirit after all? Paul gives us some clue to his meaning by relating the visible union with Christ to the sacrament of baptism, which has an obvious visibility about it: "In one spirit we have all been baptized into one body . . ." (1 Cor 12:13). "All you who have been baptized into Christ have put on Christ" (Gal 3:27). Likewise in 1 Cor 10:1-4, Paul uses the Old Testament exodus imagery as the counterpart of Christian baptism: "All were baptized into Moses in the cloud and in the sea." The Christian fulfillment, which is only partially explicitated in the sequence of this text, is that Christians were baptized into Christ in the cloud of the Spirit and the sea of the baptismal waters. At any rate, the sacrament of baptism brings to visibility and bodiliness the belonging to Jesus Christ achieved by faith and the Holy Spirit.

The same may be said for the Eucharist, although Paul envisages its function more in terms of bringing the Christian community as such to the same kind of visible manifestation: "Because the bread is one, we the many are one body, for we all partake of the one bread" (1 Cor 10:17). Similarly in the Christianized exodus imagery, as all who were baptized into Moses ate the same spiritual food (the manna) and all drank the same spiritual drink (the water from the rock), so Christians are nourished by the same spiritual food and drink from Christ. But we are here already anticipating some of the community dimension of Paul's body-theology, which must be developed in its own right further on.

The sacraments, however, are not merely external rituals. They are an incorporation into the two-fold paschal mystery of the body of Christ, namely death and resurrection. Baptism is first of all a contact with the death of Christ. Christians have died through the body of Christ (Rom 7:4f.). More graphically, "Do you know that all of us who have been baptized into Christ Jesus were baptized into his death? We were buried with him by baptism into death . . ." (Rom 6:3f.). "We have been united with him in the likeness of his death" (Rom 6:5). The Greek word *symphytoi* evokes the image of limbs of a tree which have grown together and thus share intimately the same life. The event of Christ has been for the Christian as radical as the death of Christ was for him — belonging to Christ means appropriating his death.

At the same time and inseparably, the power of Christ's Resurrection has poured into the Christian by reason of the very same baptism (Rom 6:4-11). Similarly: "One has died for all; therefore all have died. And he died for all, that those who live might live no longer for themselves but for him who for their sake died and was raised" (2 Cor 5:14,15).

Union in Life-Giving Suffering

The corporateness and visibility of the mystery, however,

also appears in the experience of suffering in the Christian life. Paul's body is the place where the paschal mystery of the death and the Resurrection of Christ are both manifested, and the context indicates that Paul is speaking about his sufferings in the apostolate: "Always carrying in the body the death of Jesus, so that the life of Jesus may also be manifested in our bodies" (2 Cor 4:10). The result is not simply the manifestation of the life of Jesus through the weakness of the body (vs. 7,11), but the awakening of new life in the communities for whom Paul spends himself (2 Cor 4:12).

Thus the solidarity suggested by the term *body* means, on the one hand, a solidarity with Christ in his death and life, but on the other hand also a solidarity with other members of the Christian community, so that the suffering and persecution of one may bring life to others, just as in the case of Jesus himself.

Embodiment in the Christian Life

Finally, the bodily union of the Christian with Jesus is also made visible through the transformation of the Christian's moral life (the meaning of "Glorify God in your body" in 1 Cor 6:20). The Christian moral life too reflects the mystery of death and resurrection — death to sin and living the new life of the resurrection. Sometimes, this is presented as a death to self, a crucifixion of the flesh (Rom 6:2,6; Gal 5:24), sometimes it is presented as living the new life of the resurrection (Rom 6:4), sometimes under both aspects at once: "So you must also consider yourselves dead to sin and alive to God in Christ Jesus" (Rom 6:11). At times the living of the new life is not called the life of the resurrection but simply the life of the Spirit (Gal 5:16-25) and the process that of sanctification (1 Thes 5:23). Paul exploits every possible approach to make it clear to the Corinthians that the Spirit of which they boast comes *from* the body of the risen Christ and moves *toward* a transformation of their bodies into his image (2 Cor 3:18; Phil 3:21).

The Body as the Community

Paul has directed the Corinthian Spirit-enthusiasm to the Body of Christ in the sense of the risen humanity of Christ and in terms of the Christians' individual body. There is a third way in which Paul seeks to give "somatology" to this "pneumatology." The Spirit is the life of the body which is the community, and the Spirit's activity aims at building up this community in love. The image under which Paul first introduces the Spirit's function in this regard is that of the temple: "Do you not know that you are God's temple and that God's Spirit dwells in you? If anyone destroys God's temple, God will destroy him. For God's temple is holy, and that temple you are." (1 Cor 3:16-17). The temple of God here is not the body of the individual Christian as it is in 6:19 but rather the community itself. And the sin against God's temple which Paul is treating here is not the sin of fornication but the sin of rivalry and disunity which threatens the very existence of the temple. Paul's theology of the divine indwelling is first of all a communitarian theology. God's temple is the community, and individuals share in the divine presence in the measure in which they are intimately united to this community and seek its unity.

The image of the temple easily lends itself to that of the body. Paul develops both of them in terms of the individual Christian in 6:12-20. So it is not surprising that he would exploit the image of the body also to develop the theme of unity in the community. For if the image of the temple suggests the holiness of the community, that of the body lends itself to the ideas of growth and interaction. The body as image for the community is introduced first in 10:17, where the unity of the community is shown from baptism. "For

just as the body is one and has many members, and all the
members of the body, though many, are one body, so it is
with Christ. For by one Spirit we were all baptized into one
body — Jews or Greeks, slaves or free — and we were all
made to drink of the one Spirit" (RSV). Note in this text
that the problem is not how the many can be one but just
the reverse — how the one Christ can be many. By reason of
Christian baptism the one Christ becomes many, and the one
Spirit becomes shared by all. From this unity of origin Paul
draws an important corollary: variety in the body is no
threat to unity but a very condition of it. This thought is developed in 12:14-26, the whole purpose of which is to show
"that there may be no discord in the body, but that the
members may have the same care for one another. If one
member suffers, all suffer together; if one member is honored,
all rejoice together" (1 Cor 12:25f. RSV).

The visible ministries in the Church are simply one of the
ways in which this common care is structured (12:27-31).
Their purpose is not the promotion of individualism, however
spiritual, but the upbuilding of the community: "Let all
things be done for edification" (1 Cor 14:26). If this edification is the purpose of all the gifts, it is above all the function of love, for the gifts without love only "puff up," whereas
love can only "build up" (1 Cor 8:1). Love, therefore, has
the role of directing the use of all the gifts to the building up
of the community. Thus Paul interrupts his long disquisition
on the gifts of the Spirit in the community to discuss the role
of love in chapter 13. He shows the essential relationship of
love to the gifts by proposing the extreme and absurd situation in which the gifts would be exercised without love (13:
1-3).

In the Corinthian community charity had been lost from
view because of an excessive affirmation of one's rights and
freedom as a Christian. In the matter of eating food that had

been offered to idols a number of the Corinthians, like Paul himself, had an enlightened conscience and thus knew that even if some meat bought in the market had previously passed through a religious ceremony in a pagan temple it was not thereby endowed with a taboo. However, other Christian converts from paganism were not so readily able to free themselves from the long engrained association of such food with pagan idolatry, and their consciences would not allow them to run the risk of eating such foods. The "enlightened" or "strong" Corinthians apparently were imposing their own "freedom in Christ" upon those less enlightened and thus were leading them to violate their own consciences in the matter. This situation wrings from Paul one of the most impassioned pleas for the right use of knowledge in the Christian community. It is not enough to be right. The delicacy of love and concern for the brother for whom Christ died presides over all, even over the use of one's own enlightenment. Such is the theme which Paul develops at great length in chapters 8, 9 and 10. Thus again the Spirit is obedient to the needs of the body. The Spirit may aim at putting the *flesh* to death, but it loves and ministers to the *body*. For this body, even in its humblest members, is the body of the risen Lord Jesus. It is not to be jettisoned but transformed into his glorious body (2 Cor 3:18).

The letters to the Corinthians have revealed new insight about Paul's spiritual theology. His theology of the origin, function and purpose of the Spirit is deeply rooted in his theology of the *body*. In some sense we might truly say that he wants to tame the Spirit for the body. The body of the Risen Lord Jesus is the source of the Spirit for the Church. The individual Christian's body is an essential part of Christ's redeeming activity. And the Spirit is given to build up all of Christ's members into his body through love. If existence in Christ is a new creation (2 Cor 5:17), then God's judgment that it is good even in its material element (Gen 1) holds as much for the new creation as it did for the first creation, and the process of redemption means a restoration of all things in Christ (cf. Eph 1:10). This will happen when the Spirit has not annihilated or escaped the body but transformed it.

Chapter Five

"THE FREEDOM WE HAVE IN
CHRIST JESUS" (Gal 2:4)

Suggested readings: Acts 20:1, 2; The Letter to the Galatians

TOWARD the end of the war Paul was waging on the western front against the false gnosis and individualism in Corinth, he had to wage another to the east. Deep in Asia Minor the churches of Galatia were being unsettled by Judaizing elements urging a return to circumcision and other observances of the Jewish law. Judging from the violence with which Paul reacts to the Galatian problem, he considered it much more dangerous than the Corinthian crisis. Most of the problems at Corinth were not problems of faith but problems of morals. But in the churches of Galatia the crisis touched the very nature of the Christian faith: is Christianity essentially Jesus Christ or the law? The situation triggers a development in Paul's theology which leads him to a deeper understanding of his own experience of freedom as a Christian and prepares for the more thorough development in Romans on justification by faith. We shall therefore draw also on the epistle to the Romans for the light it casts on Paul's understanding of Christian freedom.

Paul's exasperation with the Galatians appears from the beginning of the letter (1:6), by his conviction that he has already been through all of this before — and settled it — with the Church in Jerusalem. There the charter of freedom from the necessity of circumcision was proclaimed for the gentiles, and not even Titus who was with Paul at the time, was compelled to be circumcised (2:3). The only expectation laid upon Paul was that he should be mindful of the poor. But later Paul would have to call even Peter and Barnabas back to the simplicity of this view and its implications (2: 11-14).

The Paradox of the Law

At our distance of nearly two thousand years and our lack of familiarity with Jewish and rabbinical argumentation, we should not be surprised if we find it extremely difficult to sort out exactly what Paul means by the law and what he means by freedom from it. There are, on the one hand, those texts of Paul which condemn the law. It is a curse (Gal 3: 13), it holds man captive (Rom 7:6) or keeps man in the state of slavery (Gal 4:3), it does not justify (Gal 2:16) but brings wrath instead (Rom 4:15) and is the source of death (Rom 7:10). It is the power of sin (1 Cor 15:56) for without it man would not have known sin (Rom 7:7) and with it comes the reckoning of sin (Rom 5:13) and even the increase of trespass and sin (Rom 5:20; 7:8,13).

And yet in the same breath Paul can say that the law is holy, just and good (Rom 7:12f.), it is spiritual (Rom 7:14) it is not sin (Rom 7:7) nor is it opposed to the promises of God (Gal 3:21), for it promises life (Rom 7:10).

The resolution of this paradox will lead us to the very heart of Paul's understanding of Christian freedom. There are some Pauline texts which give us a hint of the direction in which the solution can be found. In Gal 3:24 Paul personifies the law as our "guardian" who took care of us while we were children until the age of maturity when Christ came. In the Greek social system the *paidagogos* was a slave who accompanied the child to school. Thus the law was for the period of childhood a passing experience of slavery whose purpose was to lead to Christ, the teacher. Once in the presence of Christ, the law is no longer needed.

But in itself this could hardly be a very helpful image for those Jewish Christians who had grown up finding their salvation in the observance of the law and who still felt the inner compulsion to make it the focus of their efforts. In Chapter 7 of Romans Paul describes what it is like to make the law the measuring stick of one's "justification." In this passage Paul is not describing his present psychological experience as a Christian but his previous experience as a Pharisee which he considers typical of anyone who strives to live by law. The problem is not with the law, he says, but with me (Rom 7:14), for the law, making the good all the clearer and more demanding, only increases my responsibility and guilt when I do not follow it. Thus the law is the occasion of greater sin (Rom 7:8) or through the law sin becomes "sinful beyond measure" (Rom 7:13). When Paul makes the curious statement that the law was added (to the promise) to bring about transgressions (Gal 3:19), it must be remembered that Paul, like all other biblical authors, makes no distinction between God's direct and permissive will. The law's purpose was to stop crime, but its inevitable effect was to "multiply" transgressions of the legal prescription, since an offense is no longer merely something wrong in itself but also a transgression of an express prohibition (this is the meaning in Romans 4:15; 5:13,20). Now to submit to the rite of circumcision is to take upon oneself the regime of law and to submit oneself to God's judgment on the basis of keeping the whole law (Gal 5:3; 3:12; Lev 18:5; Rom 10:5). But since even those who received circumcision do not themselves keep the law (Gal 6:13) the law thereby becomes a curse (Gal 3:13). Another way of saying this, particularly in Romans, is that man is under the wrath of God (Rom 1:18; "children of wrath" Eph 2:3), a state which involves the Jew as well as the pagan (Rom 1:18). In Galatians Paul prefers to call this state slavery (4:3,8).

Freedom in the New Covenant

Even though Paul is highly innovative in his assessment of the law, it is Jewish concepts primarily which he is using even to innovate. There was a time when scholars sought for an understanding of Paul's theology of freedom in the Greek word *eleutheria*. Scholars today are tending more and more to see the concept as a refinement of a basically Jewish idea.

In the Old Testament deliverance and freedom were habitually associated with the primordial saving act of the exodus and with the Sinai covenant, prototype and guarantee of the future saving acts of the Lord. In the exodus the Lord delivered his people from slavery. The legislation granting special consideration to slaves in Israel was intended as a permanent reminder of gratitude for this liberation (Deut 15:12-18). In the covenant the Lord bound Israel to himself, taking their future as his own and pledging that if they remained his faithful people, he would give them the land (the "heritage of Yahweh"), fruitfulness and prosperity, peace and security from foreign powers. In the covenant lay the gift of freedom (Lev 26:3-13). Falling from the covenant and the Lord meant a return to slavery (Hos 9:1-6; Jer 2:14-19; Neh 9:16f.,26f.,36f.).

This Jewish background helps us to understand why Paul finds Christian freedom fundamentally in the new exodus which is God's eschatological saving act, and in the new covenant. Watch for this — as well as for Paul's innovative understanding — in 2 Cor 3:1-18:

Am I beginning to speak well of myself again? Or do

I need leters of recommendation to you or from you as others might? You are my letter, known and read by all men, written on your hearts. Clearly you are a letter of Christ which I have delivered, a letter written not with ink but by the Spirit of the living God, not on tablets of stone but on tablets of flesh in the heart.

This great confidence in God is ours, through Christ. It is not that we are entitled of ourselves to take credit for anything. Our sole credit is from God, who has made us qualified ministers of a new covenant — a covenant not of the letter but of the spirit. The letter kills, but the Spirit gives life.

If the ministry of death, carved in writing on stone, was inaugurated with such glory that the Israelites could not look on Moses' face because of the glory that shone on it (even though it was a fading glory), how much greater will be the glory of the ministry of the Spirit? If the ministry of the covenant that condemned had glory, greater by far is the glory of the ministry that justifies. Indeed, when you compare that limited glory with this surpassing glory, the former should be declared no glory at all. If what was destined to pass away was given in glory, greater by far is the glory that endures.

Our hope being such, we speak with full confidence. We are not like Moses, who used to hide his face with a veil so that the Israelites could not see the final fading of that glory. Their minds, of course, were dulled. To this very day, when the old covenant is read the veil remains unlifted; it is only in Christ that it is taken away. Even now, when Moses is read a veil covers their understanding. "But whenever he turns to the Lord, the veil will be removed." *The Lord is the Spirit, and where the Spirit of the Lord is, there is freedom.* All of us, with faces unveiled, reflecting as in a mirror the glory of the Lord, are being transformed into that very image, from one degree of glory to another, in a way that only the Lord can do, who is Spirit (NAB except for v. 18).

In the opening lines, Paul is referring to certain Christian opponents who had sought to prove their apostolic authority by displaying a letter of recommendation from the community in which their deeds were related (3:1 with 12:11ff.). Paul responds that he needs no such letter, for the community itself is a letter which Christ has written not with ink but with the Spirit of the living God, not on tablets of stone but on tablets of the human heart (3:2,3). Paul is here clearly evoking the inward nature of the new covenant as it had been foretold by Jeremiah (31:33) and Ezekiel (36). But in vs. 6 Paul sharpens the contrast in a way that was not foreseen either by Jeremiah or Ezekiel. He describes the new covenant as a covenant "not of the letter but of the spirit," and goes on to say, "for the letter kills but the Spirit gives life." The Old Testament could say that the Spirit gives life, but it could never say that the letter kills.

In vss. 7-18 Paul pursues the contrast of the two covenants specifically in terms of glory, and he uses Ex 34:29-35 to help him do so. Both Moses and the ministers of the new covenant have been exposed to divine glory. The glory of Moses was a temporary one, and it faded with time. The glory of the new covenant is meant to last. Moses veiled his face because of the glory, but Paul sees in this veiling an attempt by Moses to forestall the disappointment of the Israelites when the glory would fade. And this suggests that the veil was really a mental block which the Israelites had and which Paul says endures to this day. When the law is read in the synagogue the veil remains over the writings as over the hearts of the Jews. In vs. 16 Paul is adapting to his purpose Ex 34:34. Whenever Moses turned to the Lord, he lifted the veil. Applying this to Israel and more specifically to their hearts, Paul says that when they turn to the Lord Jesus the veil will be lifted. In vs. 17 the Lord is the Risen Jesus, and he is the Spirit in contrast to the letter (see 3:6). But then in the second part of the verse Paul's thought advances. Having mentioned the Spirit, he speaks of the "Spirit of the Lord," that is, the Spirit given by the Lord as the initial gift to all the baptized. Since this Spirit transcends the letter of the old law both in objective revelation and in subjective experience, it brings freedom from the limitations of the law. And one of the ways in which those limitations are transcended is seen in the progressive restoration of the divine image who is Christ himself, the new Adam. Thus implicitly the Christian shares in the freedom of the new Adam.

The Promise to Abraham

If the Jewish notion of freedom was rooted in the Moses traditions, it had even deeper roots in the Abraham tradition. By New Testament times it was common among the Jews to say that they were free because they were children of Abraham: "We are descendants of Abraham. We have never been slaves to anyone!" (John 8:33). Paul too is aware of this tradition. If he used the Mosaic covenant traditions to *contrast* the superiority of freedom in Christ, he used the more congenial Abraham tradition to *illustrate* it. Abraham is Paul's preferred prototype of the covenant relationship, for the patriarch embodies the superiority of faith in the promise over mere observance of the law (Gal 3:15-18; Rom 4:13-25). When it comes to developing what this means for freedom, Paul uses the account of Abraham's begetting Isaac, the child of promise, from Sarah, the free woman, mother of the free Jerusalem (Gal 4:21-31). He calls on descriptions already given by Second and Third Isaiah of enslaved and freed Jerusalem (Isa 40:2; 52:2; 54:1-16; 60:10-14; 61:1ff.) to show how the Jerusalem which Sarah typifies is the mother of free-born children. Second and Third Isaiah tell us concretely what freedom in the new Jerusalem means. It is living in the Lord's land and experiencing his blessings, peace with the Lord and with other dwellers in the land, deliverance from oppressors, and material prosperity. All of this Paul sees fulfilled in a spiritual way in Christ and in the Church. And so the promise made to Abraham is fulfilled.

But it is fulfilled also beyond expectations. Without saying so explicitly, Paul's interpretation of the fulfillment is one that vastly transcends the hopes cherished by the children of Abraham — in more ways than one.

Sonship and Inheritance Experienced

First, as to the meaning of sonship. Though the idea of sonship retains the relationship to Abraham as father, thus assuring the freedom and the inheritance as his sons ("You are the offspring of Abraham, heirs according to the promise," Gal 3:29), the "father" to whom Christians are related is not really Abraham but God himself: "You are, in fact, all children of God through faith in Christ Jesus" (Gal 3:26).

Secondly, as to the meaning of the inheritance. In the earliest stratum of the Abraham tradition, the inheritance meant the land and all the blessings accompanying it. Later Jewish tradition understood this to extend to the "kingdom of God" which was to come. We might expect Paul to have simply connected this spiritualized hope to the promise of heavenly glory with Christ in the future kingdom. He does so in Rom 8:17. But for the Galatian situation such a future emphasis apparently would put off too much the possession of the promise. Paul is at pains to show how the promise has already been fulfilled in the present. And that fulfillment is the Holy Spirit!

To see this, one need only consider Paul's argumentation in Gal 3:2-14. It is framed by two references to the Holy

Spirit (technically, an *inclusion*) which make it clear that the Spirit already experienced in the community is the fulfillment of the promise made to Abraham, the sum of all the good things God has promised (cf. Mt. 7:11 and Lk 11:13). In 3:2-5 he asks: "Did you receive the Spirit by works of the law, or by hearing with faith? . . . Does he who supplies the Spirit to you and works miracles among you do so by works of the law, or by hearing with faith?" That is, just as faith enters into possession of the promise, so it enters into possession of the Spirit. After a long argumentation to illustrate this point, Paul concludes that the redemptive act in Christ was done "so that in Christ Jesus the blessing of Abraham might come upon the Gentiles, that we through faith might receive the promise which is the Spirit" (3:14). The parallelism here shows that Paul understands the "promised Spirit" to be, in fact, the blessing upon the Gentiles promised to Abraham. Or, to put it in another way, as Christ "received the promised Holy Spirit from the Father" (Acts 2:33), so those united with him by faith receive the same promised Spirit, the inheritance fulfilled beyond expectations.

The third way in which fulfillment transcends expectation results from the combination of the first two: it is the *experience* of sonship. And here the letter to the Romans goes beyond Galatians. In Galatians Paul argues from sonship to the Spirit: "Because you are sons, God has sent the Spirit of his Son into our hearts . . ." (Gal 4:6). This is because, using the promise made to Abraham as his basis, he argues from sonship to the consequent inheritance which is the Spirit: "If a son, then an heir" (Gal 4:7). With this established, however, he can in Romans move from the gift of the Spirit to the experience of sonship and freedom — for he is not speaking there so much of the initial gift of the Spirit but of the ongoing activity of the Spirit in one's life: "All who

are led by the Spirit of God are sons of God . . . The Spirit
bears united witness with our spirit that we are sons of God"
(Rom 8:14-16). Could it be then that Paul sees the inheritance, ultimate fulfillment of the promise made to Abraham,
in the *intimate experience of God as Father?* Yes, that is
precisely what emerges from the full text of Rom 8:14-17:

> All who are led by the Spirit of God are sons of God.
> You did not receive a spirit of slavery leading you back
> into fear, but a spirit of sonship through which we
> cry out, "Abba" (that is, "Father"). The Spirit himself
> gives witness with our spirit that we are children of
> God. But if we are children, we are heirs as well: heirs
> of God and joint heirs with Christ. (NAB)

In the expression "heirs of God" Paul has expanded his
simple "If sons, heirs" of Gal 4:7. The inheritance is God
himself — known, experienced and addressed precisely as
"Abba!" And "joint heirs with Christ" means the Christian
shares in Christ's own experience of the Father through the
gift of the Spirit (in confirmation of vs. 15, where Jesus' own
Aramaic address of the Father is the prayer of Christians).

Freedom from the Law

And now this brings us back, full circle, to Paul's notion
of freedom. Here too there is a fulfillment beyond expectations, for this freedom for Paul means *freedom from the law.*
And for this the Jewish mind was certainly not prepared.
For even the cherished freedom of the sons of Abraham was,
in the Jewish mind, intimately connected with the observance
of the law (Aboth 6:2). But the possession of the Spirit and
the conveying of sonship has now rendered it useless: "For
the law of the Spirit of life in Christ Jesus has set me free
from the law of sin and death" (Rom 8:2) and "Where the
Spirit of the Lord is, there is freedom" (2 Cor 3:17).

That the new freedom should be also freedom from the

law was not as obvious to Paul's communities as it was for him. To meet their objections he occasionally used a tack different from the strong anti-law language he was so accustomed to. He would then adopt the vocabulary of law in a positive way to show that above the law of observance there was a higher law, which he calls "the law of Christ" (Gal 6:2), "the law of faith" (Rom 3:27) or "the law of the Spirit of life in Christ Jesus" (Rom 8:2).

Let us explain this a little. Law can be understood as the expression of the divine ideal for man, an expression that is spelled out in concrete expectations of ethical conduct. Thus described the law is fulfilled simply by observance. However, already in the Old Testament man's weakness was realized, and at least here and there it was said that the Spirit of God was needed to do all that the law requires (Ps 51:10-12; Ezek 36:27 and Qumran). In the new regime the gift of the Spirit indeed enables the just demands of the law to be met (Rom 8:4), but Paul never says that the purpose for giving the Spirit was that we might now fulfill the law. Rather "through the Spirit, by faith, we wait for the hope of righteousness" (Gal 5:5), that is, man in the Spirit and by faith is responding to a higher expectation than the law of observance. He is responding to promise and gift, which can be received only through faith. In this sense Paul speaks of this "higher law" as the "law of faith," and as far as the demands of the old law are concerned, these are fulfilled in the process but indirectly so to speak, as one focuses upon the gift in faith.

But does this not open the way to sheer license? Paul's Jewish adversaries not only thought so but said so (Rom 3: 7,8). Thus it was not sufficient simply to establish the superiority of the "law of faith." Paul had to deal realistically with this, the heaviest objection to his thesis.

First of all, Paul replies through the death of Christ and

the gift of the Spirit the just requirements of the law are now fulfilled (Rom 8:3,4) and transcended, for the fruit of the Spirit, like the effect of faith (Gal 5:6), is love (Gal 5:22). And love paradoxically guarantees the Christian's freedom by leading him to indenture himself in loving service to his brothers and sisters in the community: "For you were called to freedom, brethren; only do not use your freedom as an opportunity for the flesh, but through love be servants of one another" (Gal 5:13). Thus love not only fulfills the law (Gal 5:14) but the Spirit of love inspires a host of attitudes (love, joy, peace, patience, and the rest) which so go beyond what the law expects that "against such things the law has nothing to say" (Gal 5:22,23), that is, the law disappears as the accuser (Rom 8:1). Then Paul immediately adds: "And those who belong to Christ have crucified the flesh with its passions and desires" (vs. 24). By adding this word Paul gives his final answer to the objection concerning the danger of license: Christians are not under the law, but that does not mean they are ruled by license, for selfishness (the flesh) is put to death by reason of their union with Jesus crucified. Hence the crucified one is not the accuser as was the law (being a merely external norm) but the deliverer from sin and the flesh and their works. That is why Paul can say, "There is now therefore no condemnation for those who are in Christ Jesus" (Rom 8:1) and "Who will condemn? Christ Jesus who died, yes who was raised from the dead, who is at God's right hand and intercedes for us?" (Rom 8:34)

Now, having disarmed the objection about license, Paul takes the offensive and deals the death blow. Real sinfulness now would be precisely a return to the law ("If I build up the things I tore down, *then* I would prove myself a transgressor," Gal 2:18). For returning to the law when God has obviously done so much better for us in Christ, would be to

reject the gift of God. Thus one must die to the law in order
to live now for God (Gal 2:19).

It is no easy task, of course, to let go of one's most
cherished spiritual program, but the greater gift God offers
cannot be received without that release. And the dimension
of God's new initiative as gift is portrayed most pathetically
in the death of Jesus upon the cross. The cross of Christ is
the supreme divine affirmation of gift over performance-
demand in the new regime: "I have been crucified with
Christ; it is no longer I who live but Christ who lives in me;
and the life I now live in the flesh I live by faith in the Son
of God, who loved me and gave himself up for me. *I do
not reject the gift of God as useless; for if justification comes
through the law, then Christ died in vain.* O foolish Galatians!
Who has bewitched you before whose eyes Jesus Christ was
publicly portrayed as crucified?" (Gal 2:20-3:1). Thus the
cross of Jesus, by implication, is not only the great act of
deliverance in an objective sense but is also the invitation to
enter into the experience of gift, and that is an experience of
freedom which Paul never knew before he became a Christian.

"He loved me and gave himself up for me!" (Gal 2:20).
Here is the ultimate source of Christian freedom: God is
love, and he has shown that love in a magnificent self-gift.
And that love guarantees victory over every counter-force.
*I am free because I am victorious; I am victorious because I
am loved*: "Who shall separate us from the love Christ has
for us? Shall tribulation or distress or persecution or famine
or nakedness or peril or the sword? . . . No, in all these
things we are more than conquerors through him who loved
us. For I am sure that neither death, nor life, nor angels, nor
principalities, nor things present, nor things to come, nor
powers, nor height, nor depth, nor anything else in all creation, will be able to separate us from the love God has for
us in Christ Jesus our Lord" (Rom 8:35-39).

Chapter Six

THE JUSTICE AND THE LOVE OF GOD

Suggested reading: The Letter to the Romans.

BY the time Paul reached Corinth during his third missionary journey his dispute with the Galatians, his struggle with the many problems in Corinth, and his own sufferings, had brought about a crystalization of his understanding of the gospel. He took what leisure he could find to work out his emerging synthesis in a long letter addressed to the community in Rome. He had as yet never been there, and hence he was not writing back to a community he had founded. The extent to which his letter was occasioned by groups of "the weak" or "the strong" in the Roman community to whom Paul alludes in Chapters 14 and 15 has been discussed a great deal lately among the scholars. But surely the resolution of any conflicts between these groups is not the major focus of this letter, or he would not have waited so long to introduce his considerations about them. The letter to the Romans really rises above individual conflicts and even individual communities and considers the vast sweep of God's saving plan in Christ, particularly as it touches the confluence into the one Church of the two great religious cultures of the New Testament world, the Jews and the gentiles. Paul is planning to begin his ministry in the West, and he hopes to use Rome as a springboard to Spain (15:28). This letter will introduce him to the Roman community by giving them an illustration of his teaching. It is likely that Paul's reputation has already reached Rome, with a probable effect that some of the Roman community are delighted with the prospect of his visit, and others frightened.

There are various ways of getting to the core of this letter, but the one which seems most fruitful to us is to consider the two major pillars on which the letter is built — the *justice of God* developed in 1:16-4:25 (with a flashback in 5-7) and the *love of God* introduced in the first part of chapter 5 and then developed at great length in chapter 8 on the Holy Spirit as the hope and guarantee of final victory.

The Justice of God

"Justice" as an attribute of God would hardly seem to us an attractive way to introduce the good news, for to the modern mind it seems to suggest the opposite of love and mercy. It is often associated with vindictive judgment or at any rate with the scenario of the court room, which modern man seeks to avoid as much as did his ancient counterpart. Yet it is precisely in terms of God's justice that Paul describes the gospel: "In it the justice of God is revealed" (Rom 1:17).

What has come over Paul, that he who has introduced the good news in so many other ways (as we know from his previous epistles) should suddenly leap upon the "justice of God" as a most fascinating and powerful way to present his message? The answer is not far to seek, for, as we saw in the preceding chapter, he has been led into conflict with the Judaizers over the questions of what is necessary for justification (that is, being set at rights with God). Paul had fought tooth and nail to make secure his teaching that it is faith in the saving act of God in Jesus Christ rather than the works of the law (particularly circumcision) which appropriates "justification." He now seeks to find a home for this theology of grace in God himself as he is known from the

Old Testament. And from the vocabulary of "justification" Paul's mind leaps quickly to that of the "justice of God."

"The justice of God" is a concept which, while never losing its forensic roots, means something much broader than the courtroom might suggest, indeed something truly marvelous about the ways of God. When Deborah sings of Israel's defeat of the Canaanites at the Wadi Kishon she praises "the just deeds of the Lord, his just deeds that brought freedom to Israel" (Jgs 5:11). A great act of divine deliverance is thus called "a just deed" of the Lord. Later in the Old Testament the justice of God is closely associated with his salvation. "There is no just and saving God besides me" (Isa 45:21). "I am bringing on my justice, it is not far off, my salvation shall not tarry" (Isa 46:14; see also Isa 51:5). "My salvation is about to come, my justice about to be revealed" (Isa 56:1). In Ps 69:25-28, the Psalmist prays that his enemy may have no share in God's justice. The only possible meaning that justice could have in this case is something equivalent with salvation, as appears frequently in the Psalms (Pss 40:10; 22:23, 28,31,32; 36:7). Thus, the revelation of God's justice is the revelation of his salvation: "The Lord has made his salvation known: in the sight of the nations he has revealed his justice" (Ps 98:2f.). This same sense of God's justice is found in the extra-canonical Book of Jubilees (1:5f., 15; 10:3; 31:25) and Qumran's *Manual of Discipline* (11: 13-15; 1:21; 10:23).

In Paul's introductory definition of the gospel in Romans we find the very same connection of justice and salvation along with the idea of revelation as in Psalm 98. For the gospel is first called the "power of God unto salvation" and then "in it the justice of God is revealed." The surprise that we experience in Paul's equation of justice with salvation leads us to ask why he called it justice rather than mercy or love or redemption, terms which he does use elsewhere. The immediate occasion, of course, as we have already noted, was the dispute about justification. But the equation of the justice of God with his salvation can be understood only in the light of election and covenant. The God of Israel was the God of the exodus who had chosen this people and bound himself to them in covenant: "You shall be my special possession, dearer to me than all other people" (Ex 19:5; cf. Jer 31:31ff.). He is also the God of Abraham, of Isaac and of Jacob as also of David. To each of these he made promises, and thus when he fulfills those promises he reveals himself as just to his word. In other words, the redemption in Jesus Christ is not simply an act of divine mercy but the fulfillment of a promise. Thus 1:17 could be interpreted to read: For in the gospel the promises of God are revealed as fulfilled, from the faith of Abraham who first believed in the promise to come, to the faith of Christians who believe and receive the fulfillment of that promise." And all of this despite the enormous tide of infidelities which came between in the history of Israel. But strangely enough, God's' justice is not limited to the view of simply rewarding the observance of the covenant and punishing its infractions. Rather his justice is rooted in his loving choice of Israel and his own fidelity to his people despite their sinfulness. For this reason God's justice is not to be equated with his wrath — frequently it is expressly contrasted with it (Ex 15:7,8,13; Mic 7:9; Ps 85:5,6,12,14; Dan 9:7-18). It is, in Paul's view, quite simply God's fulfillment of his promise. Since the great act of his justice is the giving of a promised gift, it cannot be received by the observance of law as man's own effort to prove himself just before God but only by acceptance of that gift actually given, just as Abraham accepted it in promise — and that attitude is faith. Now, although the justice of God manifested itself in various historical ways in the Old Testament, including victory on the battlefield, in Paul it is directed uniquely to the forgiveness of sins (3:25) and the restoration in man of the glory of God (3:23).

The Wrath of God

To show that this was indeed man's most fundamental need Paul spends a long section (1:18-2:20) showing that man, whether pagan or Jew, was alienated from God and that the regime of law, whether for pagan or for Jew, was of no benefit to him but only made matters worse. This state of need on man's part is described as his being under God's *wrath*. Lest we too easily associate this primitive term with the kind of arbitrary and vindictive wrath characteristic of the gods of the pagan myths, it is important to see the biblical context.

It is, first of all, different from the saving justice of God. It is that from which God's saving justice delivers. Far from being the effect of a mood-swing in God, it is a state in man which results from deliberately turning from a God who has revealed himself in the created universe (1:18-23). The results of this culpable turning away, though described in the biblical language of "God delivering them up" (vs. 24), are, in the last analysis, only the natural effects of their action — moral chaos and perversion of the moral conscience (1:23-32). Thus the wrath of God is essentially man's self-imposed alienation from a good God. As long as he clings to his sin, man can experience God only as *wrath*. This is Paul's meaning in 1:18: what reveals the wrath of God is the disastrous effects of man's turning from him. Paul is speaking here as a Jew thoroughly imbued with the Old Testament: "At the wrath of the Lord of hosts the land quakes and the people are like fuel for the fire" (Isa 9:17). This image of Isaiah is then interpreted not as some natural catastrophe but as the very sinfulness of the people: "No man spares his brother, each devours the flesh of his neighbor"

(Isa 9:18). Note a similar thought in Job 4:8,9: "Those who plough for mischief and sow trouble reap the same. By the breath of God they perish, and by the blast of his *wrath* they are consumed." In the biblical view sin is its own punishment and the evil God brings on sinners is primarily allowing their own schemes to bear their rotten fruits (Jer 2:19; 6:19; Hos 11:6; Prov 1:31; 26:27; Wis 11:16; 12:23,27):

> As a stone falls back on him who throws it up,
>   so a blow struck in treachery injures more than one.
> As he who digs a pit will fall into it,
>   and he who lays a snare is caught in it,
> Whoever does harm will be involved in it,
>   without knowing how it came upon him . . .
> The trap seizes those who rejoice in pitfalls . . .
> *Wrath and anger are hateful things,*
>   *yet the sinner hugs them tight* (Sir 27:25-30, NAB).

Although Paul's description applies first to the pagan, the Jew is no better off (2:1-3:20). Though he condemns the pagan (2:1-11) and possesses God's superior revelation in the law (2:12-16) he too will be condemned if he takes the law as his justification (2:17-24). Despite circumcision (2:25-29) and the promises of God to Israel (3:1-7), the Jew, like the pagan, is a sinner, and Scripture attests to the fact (3:8-20). How then can man, experiencing the wrath of God or (its equivalent) his own sinfulness, get out of his situation and be at rights with God? Only through accepting the gift of God's justice in the person and event of Jesus Christ and thus becoming justified.

Justification

Paul develops what this means in Rom 3:21-26: the justice of God justifies the sinner. From God's viewpoint it is an absolutely free gift, from man's viewpoint it is available only by faith in Jesus Christ whom God has indicated as the propitiatory available to all who believe.

The propitiatory was the golden covering for the ark mounted by two golden cherubim, serving as the place of the divine presence (Ex 25:17-22) or the very throne of the Lord (1 Sam 4:4). From this sacred place the Lord was understood not only to make known his will (Ex 25:22) but also, on the feast of the atonement, when a priest in a liturgical rite sprinkled blood on and in front of the "propitiatory," to pardon the sins of the people (Lev 16:1-19). According to this conception, the collective sins of the people during the year made them unworthy of the divine presence and thus contaminated the dwelling place of God in the midst of the community, symbolized by the Ark. When the High Priest (who alone had access to the Holy of Holies) cleansed the propitiatory with the blood of a sacrificed animal, this was understood to give visible expression to the Lord's cleansing of his people from sin. What was done in the secret of the Holy of Holies has now been fulfilled and publicly manifested in Christ — the veil has been torn away (Mt 27:51) and the blood of Christ has shown him to be the instrument of propitiation absolving all believers from their sins and bringing back the divine presence. That is why the death of Christ upon the cross was the supreme manifestation of God's justice. He shows himself to be just by justifying him who has faith in Jesus (3:26).

It is not necessary to repeat what has already been said about justice and justification from the viewpoint of its human recipient. What is important is to focus upon the divine attribute of God's own justice to which Paul reduces the whole process in Romans. By rooting "justification" in the biblical tradition of God's "justice," Paul brings to the fore aspects of justification which Pharisaic legalism and his Judaizing opponents have all but forgotten: election, call,

promise — with all that they suggested of the utter gratuity
of the gift and yet the certainty of the fulfillment of the
promise — and consequently faith which accepts the promise
and the fulfillment. To make this connection between justification and God's justice was a stroke of theological genius.
For those of us less accustomed to think of God as our
covenant God who has sworn his fidelity to us, the discovery
of this Pauline conception of God should be refreshing and
reassuring. For Paul, to think of God as just is not to be
threatened but reassured.

The Love of God

After spending the first four chapters of Romans estab-
lishing the theological context for what has already been
done in Christ, Paul begins in chapter five to look forward
to the final goal of the Christian life, salvation. In 5:1-11 the
following elements should be noted: (1) Salvation is the
final rescue to which we look forward, confidently to be
sure, but still forward: "the glory of God" is what we still
hope for (vs. 2); "to be saved" means to be saved from the
eschatological wrath of God (vs. 9); "we will be saved"
(future) by Christ's life (vs. 10). (2) If faith is the attitude by which we accept the gift of God's justice and experience it, hope is the great virtue of the journey to salvation, giving us not only assurance of the final glory of God
(vs. 2) but also even a boasting in the midst of affliction, for
these afflictions instead of discouraging actually strengthen
hope. (3) The reason for the latter paradox is that the *love
of God* has already been poured into our hearts through the
Holy Spirit who is given to us (vs. 5).

A word about this last text. The ground for Christian hope,
that is, the certainty that the future glory will be ours, is
God's love for us. The "love of God" which is poured into
our hearts is not in the first place our love for God, as if

Paul were saying: "We know that we will get to heaven because we love God." The places in Paul where "the love of God" clearly mean man's love for God are rare (1 Cor 2:9; 16:22; Rom 8:28). But the places where the love of God means God's love for us, more specifically the Father's love or Christ's love, abound. This is surely the primary sense meant here, for to point with assurance to "our" love of God would strike a major dissonance with all that Paul has tried to establish in the preceding chapters: the new life is gift from beginning to end (6:23). This love of God was proved in the first place by the death of Christ for us when we were sinners (5:8). But what in the past was a single, definitive manifestation of God's love on the stage of history now enters the Christian's own experience. That love is not only *shown* ("depicted to your eyes," Gal 3:1); it is *poured out* into our hearts by the Holy Spirit who is given to us. Only by this double manifestation of God's love is the redemptive act complete. And the Holy Spirit, like the death of Jesus on the cross, is pure gift, yet a definitive gift (as the perfect tense used in the Greek verb "has been poured out" affirms), one whose effects are still being experienced and one which God has no intention of taking away.

From 5:12 down to the end of chapter 7 Paul halts the development he had just begun about the Christian present in order to give a further development of the past act of God already accomplished. Then in chapter 8 he picks up again what he had begun to treat in the first lines of chapter 5, namely, the present life lived with the confidence and the transforming power which is the assurance of God's love given through the Holy Spirit. The contrast of the "law of the Spirit of life in Christ Jesus" with the law which is the occasion of sin and death (8:2) is carried on through the first part of chapter 8. The new life of the Spirit brings a new approach to morality and guarantees the resurrection (8:5-

13). It brings further the intimate experience of sonship and of the fatherhood of God: "For all who are led by the Spirit of God are sons of God. For you did not receive the spirit of slavery to fall back into fear, but you have received the spirit of sonship. When we cry "Abba! Father!" it is the Spirit himself bearing witness with our spirit that we are children of God, and if children, then heirs, heirs of God and fellow heirs with Christ, provided we suffer with him in order that we may also be glorified with him" (8:14-17 RSV).

In the last part of this passage just cited Paul introduces again the mystery of suffering which characterizes the Christian present and which could conceivably be used by his adversaries to question the reality of the new life in the present. This leads to a consideration about the glory that is now hidden in us but will be revealed and the eager longing — in fact the groaning — of all creation, of the Church and even of the Spirit within, for the completion of the mystery of redemption (8:18-27). Then comes the astounding statement that "God makes everything work for the good of those who love him" (8:28). "Everything" should be taken in its broadest sense, although Paul apparently is thinking in the first place of the sufferings of the present life already mentioned in vs. 18.

This leads to the magnificent concluding hymn to the love of God, victorious over everything (8:31-39). He begins by a phrase which sums up the meaning of everything he has said so far about the Christ event: God is *for* us. The justice of God means that God is for us, and so does the love of God. Now this might seem to be obvious to the point of banality, but in the light of his Christian experience Paul now sees that his God-image as a Jew and a Pharisee had not been such. However much the Scriptures may have stressed election and promise and faith, Paul had experienced God as the publisher and enforcer of performance-expectations. And those expectations, which he calls simply the law, were "against him" to the point of being a curse, and they led to the kind of spiritual frustration which he describes at length in Rom 7:7-25. In short, the law was the great accuser, that which condemned. But now in Christ it is obvious that God is himself for us, and that he who gave up his own Son for us cannot hold back anything less (8:32). And then: "Who shall bring accusation against God's chosen ones? God, who justifies? Who shall condemn? Christ Jesus, who died or rather was raised up, who is at the right hand of God and who intercedes for us?" (Rom 8:33,34). Obviously, if God himself and Jesus Christ have no condemnation to make but are on the contrary our vindicators, then there is absolutely nothing that can win any ultimate victory over us: "Who will separate us from Christ's love for us? Trial, or distress, or persecution, or hunger, or nakedness, or danger, or the sword? . . . No, in all of these things it is we who are winning the victory, and it is an overwhelming one, because of him who loved us. For I am certain that neither death, nor life, nor angels nor principalities, nor things present nor things to come, nor powers, nor height nor depth nor anything else in all creation will be able to separate us from God's love in Christ Jesus our Lord" (Rom 8:35-39).

Thus, as the justice of God is basically his saving plan which sets the sinner aright when accepted in faith, so the love of God is the infinite and inexhaustible energy which sustains and impels the Christian on his journey. Gift of the Spirit, God's love poured into the heart of the Christian is the source of that hope that does not disappoint (Rom 5:5). The basis is here being laid for the spiritual doctrine of Eph 3:14-19, where the love of God is presented as the soil that nourishes Christian growth and the foundation which stabilizes it, as well as the object of the Christian's enduring contemplation through which alone he may attain to the "fullness of God."

The justice and the love of God meet then, in one mystery of covenant love. For just as a marriage is first founded in an elective love sealed by covenant and then grows unto maturity through love, so the justice of God has been a covenanting which has put us at rights with God by making us his own in Christ Jesus; and the love of God, poured into our hearts through the Holy Spirit, is the source which feeds the full development of that union, through thick and thin, until the full glory of the relationship is revealed in the light of the resurrection.

Chapter Seven

CHRIST, THE MYSTERY OF GOD

Suggested readings: Acts 20-28; Colossians and Ephesians.

Colossians

BETWEEN the letter to the Romans and that to the Colossians, which we are assuming here to be one of the authentic Pauline letters, Paul covers a lot of ground — and water, as Acts 20-28 shows. He returns to Palestine, is imprisoned there, appeals to Caesar, and then is taken in custody to Rome. We join most authorities who hold that the letter to the Colossians was written during Paul's Roman captivity. Colossae, a city situated about a hundred miles east of Ephesus, had first been evangelized by one of Paul's disciples, Epaphras (1:7), a native of Colossae (4:12). Probably during the long period of Paul's intense activity in Ephesus, Epaphras had been converted and then, after instruction, sent to Colossae to spread the faith there, and then on to Laodicea and Hierapolis (4:13).

The letter itself gives us some clue as to what occasioned it. As happened earlier in Galatia, the Judaizing elements were undermining the original gospel which Paul preached. They were promoting circumcision (2:11-13), abstinence from certain foods (2:16,21), the observance of feasts and sabbaths in some special way (2:16). This raised the old issue about the law, its provisional and preparatory character and deliverance from it through the cross of Christ (2:14-

17). There was a new element, however, in that these ten-
dencies now appear mixed with philosophical arguments of
a gnostic or pregnostic variety, with a curious concern for
the hierarchies of angels (2:18). The Judaism of the first
century speculated on the ministry of angels in God's
governing of the world and especially in promulgating and
seeing to the observance of the Mosaic law. Though not
expressly stated, the hierarchies of angels could provide
Jewish gnostics with a ladder of "spiritualization," a program
for progressive introduction into ever more esoteric mysteries,
with a consequent despising of the somatic element for which
Paul fought so hard in the letters to the Corinthians. As a
matter of fact, these Colossian gnostics are promoting an
excessive asceticism with the paradoxical effect of giving
free indulgence to the flesh:

> Let no one disqualify you, insisting on self-abasement
> and worship of angels, taking his stand on visions,
> puffed up without reason by his sensuous mind, and
> not holding fast to the head, from whom the whole body,
> nourished and knit together through its joints and liga-
> ments, grows with a growth that is from God. If with
> Christ you died to the elemental spirits of the universe,
> why do you live as if you still belonged to the world?
> Why do you submit to regulations, "Do not handle, do
> not taste, do not touch" (referring to things which all
> perish as they are used), according to human precepts
> and doctrines? These have indeed an appearance of
> wisdom in promoting rigor of devotion and self-abase-
> ment and severity to the body, but they are of no value
> in checking indulgence of the flesh (Col 2:18-23, RSV).

It is not primarily, however, a deviant asceticism which
occasions this letter but rather the underlying doctrinal threat
to the unique *Lordship of Jesus.* Paul's response reveals a
development of his theology of Christ, his primacy over

the cosmos of matter and spirit (hence over the angels too). The basic principles are not new (cf. 1 Cor 8:6; 10:4; 2 Cor 5:19; Gal 4:3,9; Rom 8:38f.; Phil 2:10f.), but there is a new stress now in three ways: (1) Christ's Lordship means that he has not only saved mankind but also redeemed the cosmos. (2) The role of the Church in God's plan becomes clearer — it is the body of which Christ is the "head" (1: 18), and the members "fill up" what is lacking to his sufferings (1:24) and grow with a power derived from him (2: 19). In the service of this image the baptismal mysticism is further developed (2:11-13). (3) Above all, Christ and the Church are now presented as a *mystery* to be contemplated (1:26,27; 2:2; 4:3).

Mystery

The word *mystery* is not really new to us, for Paul has used it before to describe the mystery of evil already at work in the world (2 Thes 2:7) or the mysteries which the spiritual Christian knows (1 Cor 13:2; 15:51) or speaks (1 Cor 2:7; 14:2) or of which the apostle himself is the steward (1 Cor 4:1) or, finally for the total saving mystery of Christ (Rom 11:25; 16:25; and perhaps 1 Cor 2:1, where certain important manuscripts read *mysterion*, "mystery" instead of *martyrion*, "testimony").

For a long time many scholars thought that the origin of Paul's usage of the word *mystery* was Greek, Paul having adopted the vocabulary of the Greek mystery religions in order to show their counterpart in Christ. But the word was such a commonplace in the first century that we can hardly visualize Paul rifling the libraries of the mystery cults to discover it. Today most scholars agree that the *content* of the concept reveals a Jewish background.

In the Old Testament the unspeakable privilege of standing in the divine council and knowing the secret of the heavenly assembly was given to the prophet (1 Kgs 22:19-23; Jer 23:18; Job 15:8). Amos could say that the Lord does nothing without revealing his intentions to the prophets (Am 3:7). The word *mysterion* itself occurs only in the Greek translations of those Old Testament books written after the exile. In this age of anxious questioning, particularly under the impact of persecution by the Seleucid kings, Israel tried to cope afresh with the meaning of her past, particularly the promises of the covenant and the prophets (which seemed so obviously unfulfilled in a time of persecution), and she wondered greatly about her future. The mystery of evil was already being experienced as a reality. But Israel continued to believe, now in a purer way, that the Lord of history would ultimately triumph, even if it meant wiping out the present age and starting over with "the age to come." Thus the word *mystery* was used to describe the future of the kingdom, particularly in Daniel (cf. Dan 2). But it was also used in the apocryphal literature of the period and especially in Qumran for the mysteries of divine providence and of the last times. "He has made known to me the mystery of the times, and the advent of the hours he showed me" (2 Bar 81:4). The *mystery* here revealed is the ultimate destruction of evil at the end of the world when God comes to judge. The Qumran documents speak of "mystery of his good pleasure" (1 QH Frag 3:7) and of the Teacher of Righteousness, to whom God has revealed all the secrets of the words of his servants the prophets (1 QpHab 7:1-5). In both cases the meaning is the future of Israel as decoded from the Scriptures. The Qumran community applied the word mystery to its interpretation of the law. The community, it was said, understands the mystery of the Scriptures because it has the right interpretation of the law (1 QS 11:5-8). The word is also used for cosmic mysteries (see Enoch, 2 Bar, Qumran).

Mystery and Wisdom in Paul

This is the tradition and the language Paul finds apt to respond to the Colossians, who no doubt mean by "mysteries" their secret revelations and the worship of the angels.

The battle, we will notice, is not an entirely new one. The problem of a gnostic interpretation of Christianity had already reared its head in Corinth where in response to a self-inflating gnosis, Paul had held up Christ crucified as the wisdom of God (1 Cor 1,2). At the conclusion of 1 Cor he had also spoken of the final resurrection as the revelation of a mystery — the conquest of death and sin (1 Cor 15:51-56), which will be a new creation and a triumph over all the cosmic powers (1 Cor 15:21-28). Thereafter authentic knowledge is to know Christ and the power of his Resurrection and the fellowship of his sufferings (Phil 3:10). The Christian life does indeed advance in knowledge, but it is always a clearer and more precise knowledge of the object of God's self revelation, namely Jesus Christ (Phil 1:9).

The contemplative dimension of the gospel becomes the primary one in Colossians. Early in the letter Paul writes:

> We . . . have been praying incessantly for you, asking that you be filled with a perfect knowledge of his will, in all spiritual wisdom and understanding. Thus may you live in a manner worthy of the Lord so as to please God perfectly, in every good work bearing fruit and growing in the knowledge of God (Col 1:9-11).

The kind of knowledge of which Paul first speaks here is practical — a knowledge of God's will. For the Jew this would be tantamount to knowing the law (Rom 1:17,18). Aware of this, Paul immediately adds, "in all spiritual wisdom and understanding," to suggest the role of the Holy Spirit in inspiring this knowledge of God's will. Already in the Old Testament, wisdom, originally quite secular, became, under

the influence of the prophetic movement, more and more associated with the Spirit of God. For wisdom belongs to God
in the first place (Gen 2:17; 3:5, 22; Ez 28:1-10; Bar 3:15-
38) and when it is communicated to man inwardly it makes
the wise man a successor to the prophets. In the Wisdom of
Solomon, it is expressly identified with the Spirit of God
(Wis 7:22). In saying that the effect of this inspired wisdom
is to be able to lead a life pleasing to the Lord, Paul is echoing
a long O.T. tradition (Prov 6:16; 8:7, 13; 11:20; 12:22;
Sir 1:27; 27:30; Wis 4:10, 14; 7:14, 28). Finally, it should
be noted that the knowledge of God climaxing the whole
movement of the passage is prepared for by an ethical life
pleasing to the Lord. Here too Paul joins the prophetic tradition that doing God's will leads to a knowledge of him (Jer
22:16) and the wisdom tradition that seeking the practical
wisdom God offers leads to a knowledge of him (Prov 2:2-
4). From biblical times onwards, the Christian theology of
wisdom will never lose this rootedness in the soil of practical
living. Later on in this letter this practical living, source of
knowledge, is identified as love.

Meantime, beginning in 1:15 Paul describes the object of
Christian wisdom, Christ. Many authorities think that Paul
has here taken over a hymn known in the Christian liturgy
or even a pre-Christian gnostic hymn which he has, of course,
Christianized. However that may be, two series of observa-
tions should be made: (1) Structurally, there is an obvious
parallel between the first and the second half of the hymn,
the first beginning with "He is the image of the invisible God,
Firstborn of all creation" and the second with "He is the
Beginning, Firstborn from the dead." The first creation is
paralleled by the new creation in Christ's death-resurrection.
And bridging the two "creations" there is the statement: "He
is the head of the body, the Church." If this statement is
meant to be the climax of what precedes, then Christ's head-

ship over the Church is seen by Paul to be a greater title of honor than his lordship over the cosmos. At any rate, the image of the body of Christ, already introduced by Paul in 1 Corinthians but without attributing any specific membership to Christ himself, is now enriched by relating him to the body as its head. This image will make possible the developments in Ephesians 5, where from the idea of headship over the body the thought moves to that of love and care for the bride because she is really his own body. Here, however, it is not the Church that is apotheosized (the later view of Ephesians) but rather the universal headship of Christ.

Implicit in Paul's thought is that growth and perfection mean a clear understanding and appreciation of that mystery. This is said clearly in Col 2:1-3:

> For I want you to know what a great struggle I carry on for you and for all those who have not seen me in the flesh, that they may be strengthened in heart, taught by love to know clearly, understand deeply and appreciate firmly God's mystery, Christ. In him lie hidden all the treasures of wisdom and knowledge.

There are some difficulties about this text, which should be cleared up first, and then a justification given of my translation, which is quite a free one.

The Greek word which we have translated simply "taught (by love)" can be translated, and often is, as "united, knit together (by love)". Paul uses the verb with the latter meaning in Col 2:19, and it appears again in this sense in Eph 4:16. Charity appears as the bond of perfection in Col 3:4. If that meaning is taken, then the Colossians' unity in charity is a necessary precondition for their coming to understand the mystery of Christ.

However, Paul's concern in Colossians is less the matter of unity than that of doctrinal clarity. Although the two are very closely related, they are not quite the same thing. Paul's struggle to enlighten their faith against heterodox teachings and the immediate context which has to do with enlightenment and knowledge, make it more likely that we should accept the other meaning of the Greek verb, which is the only sense in which it is used in the Septuagint (and in Acts 19:33), namely, "instructed, taught." Charity is then more than a bond. It teaches!

What is the effect of its teaching? The sequence of the text is a piling up of redundancies whose intentional purpose is to express the vastness of the object. Literally, "taught by love unto all the riches of full assurance of understanding, unto the exact knowledge of God's mystery . . ." I have tried to capture the various nuances in the simplified translation I have made.

The point most noteworthy here is that charity has a contemplative function. The more one loves, the more one understands. And also the more one loves the more one attaches himself to the mystery which contains the whole of God's revelation: Christ. There is an implicit rebuke in the last line to those who would seek wisdom and knowledge elsewhere, in the angels, in fruitless philosophical speculation, or strange ascetical practices.

Ephesians

Some of the ideas broached in Colossians receive more ample development in the so-called letter to the Ephesians — so called because it is not at all clear that the letter was addressed to the Ephesians. The words "in Ephesus" which sometimes are included in the translation of the opening address are missing from the best manuscripts. Paul moreover does not seem to be known personally to most of the readers (Eph 1:15; 4:21), and the general tone of the letter makes it more likely that it was a circular letter addressed to a number of churches in Asia Minor. It is even disputed whether Paul himself wrote the letter. Some scholars go so far as to make it a late first-century composition by someone imitating Paul's style. Against this extreme position it may be noted that if indeed someone other than Paul wrote it, he was at least so imbued with Paul's thought and style that his work is neither manifestly a spurious piece of propaganda nor on the other hand a forgery mechanically slavish to Paul's phraseology. Rather the letter in relation to Colossians is organically creative. Thus a number of scholars find the easiest solution to be that a disciple of Paul, thoroughly imbued with his thought, expanded the Christological and especially the ecclesial insights of Colossians in a general letter, which may or may not have been commissioned by Paul and may or may not have received his final approval. Our position is that Ephesians is a legitimate culmination of Paul's thought and should therefore be considered in understanding his theology. This was, at any rate, the view of the Church in receiving Ephesians into the canon.

Rooted and Founded in Love

The contemplative dimension already broached in Colossians receives even greater emphasis in Ephesians, with a clearer relation to faith and charity as the root of the refined knowledge of the mystery. For example:

> . . . I on my part, hearing of your faith in the Lord Jesus and your charity toward all the saints, do not cease giving thanks for you, remembering you in my prayers, that the God of our Lord Jesus Christ, the Father of glory, may give you a spirit of wisdom and revelation in the knowledge of himself. With the eyes of your heart enlightened, may you know what is the hope of his calling, what the riches of glory of his inheritance in the saints, and the exceeding greatness of his power toward us who believe . . . (Eph 1:15-19).

We find ourselves in the midst of a rapturous hymn where words seem inadequate to convey the wonder experienced by the author and where it may be difficult to extract the implied theology because of the almost ecstatic piling up of phrases. But let's try.

Notice first the mention of faith and charity as the foundation of the new growth Paul is going to pray for. Faith is related to the person of the Lord Jesus, vertically as it were, and love is directed "to all the saints," horizontally as it were, to the members of the Church here conceived as a universal body transcending the individual congregation. Secondly, the prayer is essentially a thanksgiving — in fact, the whole first part of Ephesians is one long *berakah,* a typical Jewish form of thanksgiving prayer. According to Paul's directive, prayers of petition should always be accompanied by thanksgiving (Phil 4:6).

Thirdly, the Father is addressed as "the God of our Lord Jesus Christ." What is meant by this expression? We could easily understand "the *Father* of our Lord Jesus Christ," and perhaps we should simply recall that *ho theos* is habitually used in the Pauline literature as meaning the Father. However, there is a sense too in which God has become in a new sense "our God" because of our belonging to Jesus Christ, as expressed in John 20:17: "I ascend to my Father and to your Father, to *my* God and to your God."

Fourthly, the mention of the "spirit of wisdom and revelation" gives the whole passage an implicit Trinitarian reference. The particular spirit-gift sought is again one of insight into the mystery of God himself, and its effect is to enlighten the heart (i.e. the Christian's whole inner being) so as to appreciate the gift given and the gift promised. "To know the hope" is obviously a knowledge of appreciation, as when one in mature life is overwhelmed by a precious gift because he knows its cost and its meaning. The object is first of all "the hope of his calling" and "the riches of his inheritance," which refer to the future. But this coupled with "the exceeding greatness of his power toward us who believe," indicating a present effectiveness in the Christian life. Or, as Heinrich Schlier has laconically commented: "Through the knowledge of the glory contained in the inheritance, the longing for it grows; through the knowledge of God's power, the certitude of attaining it."

The culmination of the *berakah* comes in 3:14-21:

> . . . I bend my knees to the Father from whom all fatherhood in heaven and on earth receives its name, that he grant you in a measure in keeping with the riches of his glory, to be strengthened with power through his Spirit, for the progress of the inner man. May Christ find a home, through faith, in your hearts; may you be rooted, then, and founded in love, so that you may be enabled to grasp, with all the saints, what is the breadth and length and height and depth, and to know Christ's love which surpasses knowledge — in order that you may be filled unto all the fullness of God.
>
> Now to him who by the power at work within us is able to do far more abundantly than all that we ask or imagine, to him be glory in the Church and in Christ Jesus to all generations, for ever and ever. Amen.

Again it is very clear that faith and love are the root and foundation of a growth in understanding the mystery. It is equally clear that there is an expectation that faith and love grow *de facto* in this contemplative dimension. It is also clear that the Father, Christ and the Spirit are all involved in this growth. But there is something distinctly new in the expression, "May Christ find a home in your hearts through faith." Paul had of course spoken in earlier letters about the Church being in Christ, or Christ being in the Church. But he had never used the Greek verb *katoikein* to express this relationship. The verb in its most literal sense means "to settle," in contrast to a sojourning type of existence expressed by another word *paroikein*. The latter was used for the kind of nomadic existence Abraham first led in the promised land (Gen 31:1; Heb 11:9). Thus the Ephesian text is speaking of a permanent indwelling as in a home, with the connotations of ownership and familiarity. But the tense of the Greek verb is aorist, and this suggests a new initiative, a new kind of coming, a new depth of "settling in." The author is not at all suggesting that Christ has never been in his people before but rather that their growth will mean his further entry into their hearts, a deeper taking of possession of them, not as guest but rather as Lord of the house, maker of the home. On the part of the recipient this is possible only through a new progress in faith, that attitude which in Pauline thought is above all receptivity to the gift of God.

Faith, of course, in Paul never stands alone, for it works through love (Gal 5:6). So here, an almost equivalent way of expressing the "deeper inhabitation" through faith is: "being rooted and founded in love." There is a typically Pauline combination of agricultural and architectural images here. Love is depicted as the soil in which the Christian is to be rooted, and implicitly the source from which he is to be fed the subsequent superior knowledge. Alternately, love is also the foundation of the edifice which will be built upon it, and that edifice, in the light of what has just been said about Christ's indwelling, is obviously a temple. In either case, there is a relationship of principle or source to fruit or culmination.

The resultant knowledge is expressed in a paradoxical way. On the one hand, the verb describing the knowing is *katalabesthai*, which means "to seize, to grasp, to comprehend." And yet the object is the four dimensions of the cosmos — obviously intended to describe the infinite reaches of the mystery. Somehow then, this knowledge born of a deeper union with Christ in faith and love enables one to comprehend the infinite. The paradox is carried on by the sequence: "and to know Christ's love which surpasses understanding." Either this knowledge is simply the experience and the confession that one is immersed in an object that can never be measured or exhausted — or this knowledge does in some way give one an understanding of what is beyond understanding: Christ's love. At any rate, love here appears not only as the source of Christian contemplation but also as the object of it. Thus the experience of the divine love appears as an endless circle. One begins with love to know; what one comes to know is love; and this in turn engenders greater love.

The author sees this rhythm or sequence of love-knowledge-love as the way in which one reaches perfection, which he expresses as being "filled with all the fullness of God." God, that is the Father, is the ultimate goal, just as he is the original source of the whole mystery (vs. 14).

The Church

The great originality of Ephesians is, however, its emphasis on the Church. Already in Colossians, of course, the Church was not absent from the "Mystery," but in Ephesians the extension of the mystery to the Church is explicit. God's plan, realized in Christ, is to unite Jew and Gentile into one new people, to make of them one new man (Eph 2:15). "To me . . . this grace was given . . . to make all men see what is the plan of the *mystery* hidden for ages in God . . . that through *the Church* the manifold wisdom of God might now be made known to the principalities and powers in the heavenly places . . ." (Eph 3:8-10). The mystery is, of course, the whole Christ event, particularly his Resurrection and exaltation which puts him above all the cosmic powers (Eph 1:21); but the *plan,* i.e., the strategy, is that this exaltation should be manifested in the Church. The existence and the growth of the Church is the realization and manifestation in time and space of Christ's victory over the cosmic powers. Hence, if there was any doubt about the relationship of the Church to the cosmic powers in our analysis of Col 1:18, there is none in Ephesians. Notice too in Eph 1:20-23 how the headship over the Church comes in a climactic position *after* the mention of the cosmic powers — not only lord of the universe but also head of the Church: ". . . the working of his great might, which he accomplished in Christ when he raised him from the dead and made him sit at his right hand in the heavenly places, far above all rule and authority and power and dominion, and above every name that is named, not only in this age but also in that which is to come; and he has put all things under his feet, and has given him to be the head over the whole Church, which is his body, the fullness of him who is attaining his cosmic perfection in all his members" (Eph 1:19-23). The Church is implicitly above the cosmic powers because, unlike them, she can claim to be Christ's very body.

Growth of the Church

Since the growth of the Church is a divine work wherein the destiny of the universe is worked out, the dynamics of its growth deserve serious consideration, and Paul addresses himself to this question beginning in chapter 4. Since the Church is basically a mystery of unity, all the energies of the Church must be mustered to this purpose. First, the energies commonly shared by all the members: the grace of the one calling, the one hope, the one Spirit, one Lord, one faith, one baptism, one God and Father of all (4:4-6). Then, even the diversity of gifts and offices in the Church is aimed at the same unity:

But to each one of us grace has been given according to the measure in which Christ has bestowed it. Thus the Scripture says: "Ascending on high, he led away captives; he gave gifts to men." Now what does this expression "he ascended" mean, but that he also descended into the lower parts of the earth? He who descended is the same one who ascended above all the heavens that he might fill the universe. And it was he who gave some men as apostles, others as prophets, others as evangelists, others as shepherds and teachers, so as to organize the saints for active ministry in building up the body of Christ, until we all as a whole perfectly attain to the unity of the faith and of the thorough knowledge of the Son of God, to perfect Manhood, to the mature stature that befits Christ's fullness — so that we may no longer be children tossed about and swung round by every wind of teaching that cheating men contrive in craftiness that leads to the trap error has laid. Rather, by embodying the truth in love, let us grow up unto him in every respect. He is the head, Christ. From him the whole body, growing more and more compact and closely knit together through every life-feeding contact (according to the measured activity each single part deploys), the whole body, I say, works out its increase for the building up of itself in love (Eph 4:7-16).

The grace of which the author speaks here is not the grace that saves, or charity, which abound and overflow without measure (Rom 5:15, 17, 20; Eph 1:8; 1 Thes 3:12; 2 Thes 1:3; Phil 1:9), but rather the grace of ministry, which is always proportioned to the needs of the whole community (1 Cor 12: 18ff.; cf. Rom 12:6). Christ's ascension put him in a position of pouring out gifts upon the Church (the text of Ps 68:19 is tailored and accommodated to this purpose). The purpose of his Ascension was that he might "fill all things." The Greek expression for "all things" is practically equivalent to "the cosmos, the universe of matter and spirit." To this end, Christ gave to the Church certain offices. The list is not meant to be exhaustive of the gifts or the offices, but, in view of the doctrinal function implied later in the text, Paul chooses those offices having to do with authority and teaching. The apostles were those sent out either by the Lord himself or by missionary communities to preach and found new communities. Prophets were those who probably originally exercised the gift of prophecy and came to be recognized as leaders and especially inspired preachers in the community. Evangelists were itinerant missionaries. Shepherds (or pastors) were authorities set over local churches in a more permanent way. Teachers were closely associated with the shepherds as responsible for the formation of the community in the authentic tradition of the Church. All of these, however, have as their purpose, not to do all the building of the community themselves, but rather as supervisors or animators, to discover, release and direct the Church-building power latent by divine gift in every member. This interpretation is based on a proper understanding of the Greek underlying (and, in our opinion, justifying) our translation, "in order to mobilize the saints for active service in building up the body of Christ."

The term of the upbuilding of Christ's body is variously described: unity in faith — not, obviously in its object, which is one, but rather in the effective unity of the Church made by the one faith; then the thorough knowledge of the Son of God. Again we meet the Pauline expression *epignosis,* which as we have pointed out much earlier, always means an objective knowledge, a refined, more exact understanding and securer possession of an object already known. "To perfect manhood" reads literally in the Greek, "unto perfect man." Christ is the new Adam, the "new man" in whom God is

creating a new humanity. The Church reaches perfect manhood when it attains the perfection befitting Christ's "fullness."

Pleroma

The word for fullness is the Greek *pleroma*. It is a dense
and manifold concept which Paul uses as a keystone of his
theology. In the Greek world of Paul's day, "pleroma" or-
dinarily meant "fullness" in the passive sense, "that which is
filled," hence a "capacity." It was used for the hold of a ship.
Today we might use it for a container — that object whose
purpose is to hold something. But it could also at times be
used in an active sense, as a "fullness which fills." The two
usages of the concept are illustrated in the Bible by the expression, "The earth is the Lord's and its fullness" (Ps 24:1)
and, in the verb form, "Do I not fill heaven and earth? says
the Lord" (Jer 23:24). In the Stoic world the word "pleroma"
had both a cosmic and religious dimension, in the sense that
the world was conceived as a fullness, and so was God. World
and God were coterminous; God filled the world, the world
filled God. The concept among the Stoics was static and
pantheistic.

Not so for Paul. Though he could not have been ignorant
of the meaning of the word in the Hellenistic world, his use
of it shows his Old Testament and Christian roots. "Fullness"
of course applies in the first place to God (Eph 3:19), for
all perfection is in him. But inasmuch as fullness suggests
dynamic overflowing, God's fullness is always seen as an
active communication of his perfection. Christ in turn, is
God's fullness, inasmuch as God pours into him all the
"fullness of the Godhead bodily" (Col 2:9). In a passive
sense, Christ is a capacity for God. But he too is active, and
he *fills* the Church and the cosmos with his gifts (Eph 4:7-
16). The Church in turn is Christ's fullness inasmuch as she

is capacity for the life that flows from him (Eph 1:23; 4:13) and, in turn, is the instrument through which Christ fills the universe. The universe is thus the final beneficiary of the "filling" process (Eph 4:10).

One may find it helpful to picture a multi-tiered fountain in the center of a city square. As the water fills the top level, it overflows to the second, the second on filling overflows to the third, and so on. In a similar fashion God (the Father) is the source of all life and perfection. From his fullness he pours that life into Christ, Christ in turn pours it into the Church, his body, and the Church in turn makes it present to the universe. This is not a once-done action but a continually on-going one, so that the life being received from Christ is the very life being poured into him by the Father. And in the process all things are being returned to God (Eph 1:10). This is the Pauline way of describing what the Gospel of John describes in terms of the disciples' sharing the life and love perpetually circulating between Father and Son (John 14-17).

By giving the term *pleroma* dynamic, Christological and ecclesiological dimensions Paul robs it of its Stoic pantheism and its Gnostic individualism and makes it serve a truly redemptive re-creation.

Dynamics of Growth

Returning now to the text of Ephesians 4:15, the author first shows the negative effect of this process in the Church: it gradually removes the dispersal of energies caused by false teaching. Then in vs. 16 the positive program for the growth of the Church is capsulized in the cryptic phrase: "By embodying the truth in love." The Greek *aletheuontes* is sometimes translated, "speaking the truth" (a meaning the verb has in Gal 4:16). But here the word is simply the participial form of the noun *aletheia*, "truth." And by "truth" much more is meant than veracity. "Truth" stands for the whole context of the Christian message as well as the kind of life it calls for. Thus "truthing it in love" is very akin to John's expression, "doing the truth" (Jn 3:21; 1 Jn 1:6; Gen 32: 11; 47:29; Isa 26:10), which means giving the truth of the Christian faith a concrete living expression. Thus we translate, "embodying the truth." It is, again, love that gives faith its visibility (Gal 6:4). And it is love, the embodiment of the truth, that is the source of the universal growth of the Church. There is no authentic growth if it does not proceed from love. Christ is the goal ("unto him") towards whom the Church, his "complement," grows.

But he is also the source of all growth. From Christ the whole body derives its growth. The Greek expression *auxesin poietai* means that the body "makes growth for itself," the middle voice of the Greek verb indicating that the body does this for its own benefit. Thus, while Christ is the source of all growth, he endows the body with its own inward life and dynamic. What comes from Christ is appropriated and implemented by the body as its own.

And the way in which the body works for its own growth in Christ is described in another pile-up of expressions: "growing more and more compact and closely knit together through every life-feeding contact (according to the measured activity each single part deploys)" (vs. 16). There is again a mixture of architectural and organic figures here. The first expression, "growing more and more compact" evokes the entire ancient building process in which stones were rough-quarried, then smoothed so as to fit snugly together, then were prepared with dowels to interlock them, and finally built up upon one another to form a building. Suggested here is that individual members of the Church by their interaction will have to adjust to the life of the new edifice they have become and sacrifice their "rough edges" in favor of the

whole. Then the next expression "closely knit-together"
evokes organic inter-relationship, for the term is taken from
the interconnection of body-members through ligaments. This
image complements the former by suggesting that the life of
the Church is indeed an organic one and, as the sequence of
the text makes clear, when one member interacts with another, life is transmitted, not only from member to member
but also, in the process, from Christ the head. It is thus that
the body, from Christ, builds itself up in love (vs. 16).

Thus Paul's theology of spiritual growth is brought to a
grandiose climax in Ephesians with its stress on the cosmic
mystery of God's redemptive plan in Christ realized through
the Spirit in the Church. If there is less emphasis on the
parousia as the motive for Christian growth (as appeared
so strongly in the Thessalonian correspondence), there is a
correspondingly greater appreciation of the interim in terms
of the mystery of Christian becoming in the present. The age
of the Church is not so much an age of waiting as it is an
age of growth. The parousia is still thought of, but it is conceived now as the moment when Christ presents to himself
his bride, the Church, fully perfect, without spot or wrinkle
(Eph 5:27). For all that is essential in the process, this was
begun in baptism (Eph 5:26) and is continued by the feed-
ing of his body through the Eucharist (Eph 5:29). Love is
the essence of the growth (Eph 4:16), and all things in the
Church, particularly its gifts and ministries, are aimed at
building up the Church in love. Not that this insight is new
with Ephesians. In Paul's very first letter we saw love as the
central source of Christian growth. But we have also seen
how this growth in love assumed different modalities as we
followed Paul through his long ministry — how, from a rather
simple notion of doing good to one's brothers and to all men,
it more and more assumed a discerning function (in Corinthians, particularly in sensitivity to other members in the

community and then in Philippians and especially in Colossians a discerning of true doctrine from false), and finally a contemplative function in Ephesians.

Conclusion

We may then conclude our pursuit of Paul's understanding of the development of the Christian life by noting the stages: Paul turns from the law to the person of Jesus Christ (chapter 1), who is known first as the glorious coming one whose return is guaranteed by his resurrection from the dead. The Christian life is a preparation in faith, hope and love for his coming (chapter 2). Then, it is a life presently lived out in suffering, which is seen as a sharing in the mystery of Christ's death, already anticipating in joy the power of his Resurrection (chapter 3). The common life in the body of Christ is one animated by the Holy Spirit, but the Holy Spirit is the Spirit of Jesus and the Spirit of his body (whether understood as his own risen but very real humanity, or as the body of the individual Christian or as the body which is the Church), and thus the Spirit sanctifies the body and serves it through gifts and ministries (chapter 4). Since the plan of salvation is essentially God's gift to which man responds in faith, to return to the law as a way of salvation is to return to slavery after experiencing the freedom of Christ (chapter 5). God's saving purpose was indeed free but it was also fulfillment of his own promise, and thus the gospel is the announcement of his "justice" coming to justify the sinner who cannot save himself. Once justified, the Christian has the assurance of God's love to carry him victoriously through all the counterforces of this life (chapter 6). Finally, one can only sing of the incomprehensible mystery of God's plan of love in Christ and strive to live in that mystery as its riches are daily revealed more and more in the life of the Church as it grows to the fullness of Christ (chapter 7).

Epilogue

"I PREFER TO APPEAL IN THE NAME OF LOVE" (Philemon 9)

Suggested reading: The Letter to Philemon.

AFTER the grandiose cosmic panorama to which Paul's letters have led in Colossians and Ephesians, we may feel we've been on a space voyage from which, for all its beauty, we would now welcome a re-entry to earth. Granted that Christ is Lord of the principalities and powers, granted that "all things have been put under his feet," granted that by the cross he has reconciled Jew and Gentile and all things in heaven and earth — what does this cosmic vision have to say about daily living? In God's strange providence, the shortest of Paul's letters, written in prison probably about the same time as Colossians, gives us a magnificent insight not only into the person of Paul but also into the concrete meaning of his soaring theological flight in these last years of his life. It is the letter to Philemon.

Brief as it is, the letter allows us to put together the story that went before it — and because the letter was preserved by Philemon and his household, we can assume the story had the happy ending the letter itself was meant to bring about.

Philemon was one of Paul's early converts from the higher economic class. He had a home large enough to house the meetings of the Christian community in those days when "church" meant not a building but a community. He was known for his hospitality; and there was in his household at least one slave named, appropriately, *Onesimus,* "Useful." Whether Onesimus became part of Philemon's household after the latter's conversion to Christ or before, we do not know. We do know that the slave did not share his master's faith in the Lord Jesus, or that at least he did not openly profess his desire to become a Christian. More than that, relations between Onesimus and Philemon must have become strained, so that one day when the chance came, Onesimus fled the household and the country, pocketing a few things from the house, it seems, to pay for his journey. Where to go? Whether by intention or chance, he ended up in Rome visiting Paul in prison and attending to his needs.

In the course of their ministry to one another, Onesimus decided to accept Jesus as the Lord of his life, and Paul had him baptized. But now, what a delicate problem Paul had on his hands! For what about Philemon who was equally Paul's friend and brother in Christ? Would Paul stand on the liberty of the gospel and tell Onesimus that since all bonds have been broken by Christ's death and Resurrection, he should simply ignore any claims Philemon might have? And if so, should Paul keep Onesimus at his side for his own needs? Or should he send him off to some distant and anonymous Christian community where his whole past could be hidden from discovery? Or should Paul on the contrary press obedience and urge Onesimus to return to Philemon and re-enter his master's service? There would be a risk about that, for what guarantee was there that Philemon, Christian though he is, would not in this area of his life still have a pagan "blind-spot" and retaliate vindictively? In the Graeco-Roman world, masters had the right to put their own slaves to death without consulting anybody!

Whence the dilemma: Paul knew that Onesimus, like the imprisoned apostle himself, had every right to be free. And had Philemon not been a Christian, it might well have been that Paul would not have taken the risk he did. But Philemon was a Christian and Paul loved him also as a dear friend. And in the Christian community, as Paul had long ago affirmed to the Corinthians, it isn't sufficient to be right, it isn't sufficient to operate on a dynamic of win-or-lose, and it isn't Christ's way to impose his own rights on others, as one might be forced to do in the political arena. There is another dynamic, and it is trust born of love. And if that means putting one's heart freely in the hands of one's brothers and sisters, to let them do with it what they will, then so be it. "We must lay down our lives for our brothers" (1 John 3:16). Whether John understood that to mean taking the risk of trusting them to the extent of putting one's life in their hands, we do not know. What we do know is that is what Paul taught — and lived.

And so his decision was to send Onesimus back to Philemon with a letter in which Paul laid his own heart with Onesimus before his fellow Christian, requesting freedom for Onesimus — and a new freedom for Philemon.

The letter speaks for itself without commentary. It is a precious conclusion to the Pauline literature, a seal of authenticity upon Paul's whole life and work. For it shows that the gospel with all its glorious vistas was for Paul not a matter of words but a matter of love, which alone can achieve authentic reconciliation and freedom. Paul, like his own Master before him, chose to lay aside power in order to embrace in love one who might in the process impale him — but who might also in the process find the freedom to be reborn.

ANNOTATED BIBLIOGRAPHY

Bornkamm, G. *Paul* (New York: Harper and Row, 1970). The reader of this contemporary study by an outstanding Protestant scholar should not overlook the important critique of it given by C.H. Giblin in *The Catholic Biblical Quarterly* 34 (1972), 349-51.

Cerfaux, L. *The Spiritual Journey of St. Paul* (New York: Sheed and Ward, 1968). A good, less technical survey of the development of Paul and his theology.

Cerfaux, L. *Christ in the Theology of St. Paul* (1959), *The Church in the Theology of St. Paul* (1959), *The Christian in the Theology of St. Paul* (1967). This trilogy of Pauline theology published by Herder and Herder is perhaps the most comprehensive compendium available. Somewhat technical at times, it is nonetheless clear in its exposition and penetrating in its insight.

Dibelius, M. and Kümmel, W. *Paul* (Philadelphia: Westminster Press, 1953). Concise. Excellent as a presentation of Paul's response to his life-events in terms of his personal development. A number of scholars would dispute the position that Paul's sacramental theology was influenced by the mystery cults. Some of the statements on righteousness reflect the Reformation polemic.

Fitzmyer, J. A. *Pauline Theology: A Brief Sketch* (Englewood Cliffs: Prentice-Hall, 1967); reprinted from the *Jerome Biblical Commentary*. Excellent, concise overview.

Montague, G. T. *Maturing in Christ* (Milwaukee: Bruce, 1964). A readable exposition of Paul's theology of the development of the Christian life.

Montague, G. T. *The Living Thought of St. Paul* (Milwaukee: Bruce, 1966; Second, revised edition, 1976). An introduction to Pauline theology through intensive study of key texts.

Nock, A. D. *Saint Paul* (New York: Harper and Row, 1963). One of the best lives of Paul in English.